HEBREW THROUGH PRAYER

דֶּרֶךְ תְּפִלָּה

2

Terry Kaye

Karen Trager

Patrice Goldstein Mason

BEHRMAN HOUSE, INC.

The editor and publisher gratefully acknowledge the cooperation of the following
sources of photographs for this book:
Bill Aron, 5, 77; Bachman/The Image Works, 74; Sharon Faulkner, 45;
Francene Keery, cover, 41, 52; S.A.R. Academy/Devorah Preiss, 61.

Special thanks to the Society for the Advancement of Judaism for their cooperation
(photographs appear on cover and page 41).

Book Design: Itzhack Shelomi
Cover Design: Robert J. O'Dell
Cover Photo: Francene Keery
Illustrator: Jana Ben-Moshe
Project Editor: Adam Siegel

Contents

1   אָבוֹת

The heart of every prayer service is a series of blessings called the עֲמִידָה.
אָבוֹת ("fathers" or "ancestors") is the first part of the עֲמִידָה.
אָבוֹת praises יְיָ — the God of our ancestors. It also asks God to help us and to protect us just as God helped and protected our ancestors.

• • • • • • • • •

Practice reading the אָבוֹת aloud

1.   בָּרוּךְ אַתָּה יְיָ, אֱלֹהֵינוּ וֵאלֹהֵי אֲבוֹתֵינוּ,

2.   אֱלֹהֵי אַבְרָהָם, אֱלֹהֵי יִצְחָק, וֵאלֹהֵי יַעֲקֹב.

3.   הָאֵל הַגָּדוֹל, הַגִּבּוֹר וְהַנּוֹרָא, אֵל עֶלְיוֹן.

4.   גּוֹמֵל חֲסָדִים טוֹבִים, וְקוֹנֵה הַכֹּל, וְזוֹכֵר חַסְדֵי אָבוֹת,

5.   וּמֵבִיא גְאֻלָּה (גּוֹאֵל) לִבְנֵי בְנֵיהֶם, לְמַעַן שְׁמוֹ, בְּאַהֲבָה.

6.   מֶלֶךְ עוֹזֵר וּמוֹשִׁיעַ וּמָגֵן.

7.   בָּרוּךְ אַתָּה יְיָ, מָגֵן אַבְרָהָם.

Praised are You, Adonai, our God and God of our ancestors,
God of Abraham, God of Isaac, God of Jacob.
Great, mighty, and awesome God, supreme God.
God, to whom the world belongs, You do acts of lovingkindness
and recall the faithfulness of our ancestors.
You bring redemption (a redeemer) to their children's children for the sake of
Your name. God, You are our helper, and savior, and shield.
Praised are You, Adonai, the Shield of Abraham.

Prayer Dictionary

אָבוֹת
fathers, ancestors

אֵל
God

אֱלֹהֵי
God of

אֱלֹהֵינוּ
our God

אֲבוֹתֵינוּ
our fathers,
our ancestors

אַבְרָהָם
Abraham

יִצְחָק
Isaac

יַעֲקֹב
Jacob

חֲסָדִים טוֹבִים
acts of
lovingkindness

חַסְדֵי אָבוֹת
faithfulness
of the fathers,
ancestors

Search and Circle

Circle the Hebrew word that means the same as the English.

English			
Abraham	אָבוֹת	יִשְׂרָאֵל	אַבְרָהָם
fathers, ancestors	אַתָּה	אָבוֹת	אֱלֹהֵי
our God	בָּאֵלֶם	אֱלֹהֵינוּ	לְעוֹלָם וָעֶד
Isaac	יִצְחָק	אֶחָד	שַׁבָּת
Jacob	בָּרוּךְ	כָּבוֹד	יַעֲקֹב
our fathers, our ancestors	אָבוֹת	אֱלֹהֵינוּ	אֲבוֹתֵינוּ

The Jewish people feel a special responsibility to help and protect one another. These girls are dressed as giant tzedakah boxes to remind us to be generous when we give צְדָקָה. In this way, we can help feed, clothe, or house Jews less fortunate than ourselves.

A Closer Look

The אָבוֹת is a בְּרָכָה. It is the first of many blessings that make up the עֲמִידָה.

How can you tell that אָבוֹת is a בְּרָכָה?

Write the clue words. _____ _____ _____

Now write the root of the word בְּרָכָה. _____ _____ _____

This root means "bless" or "praise."

אָבוֹת ends with a second בְּרָכָה. Write it here.

_____ _____ _____ _____ _____

Family Tree

Abraham, Isaac, and Jacob are called the אָבוֹת ("ancestors") of Judaism because they were the first family to believe in one God.

Fill in the missing English words on the family tree of our ancestors.

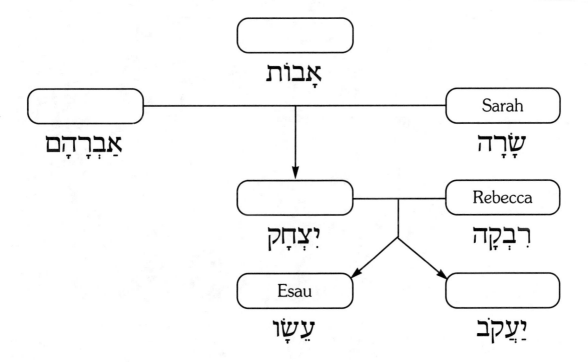

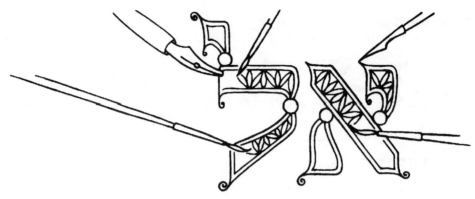

Prayer Building Blocks

אֵל "God"

. . . .

אֵל   means "God."

אֱלֹהֵי   means "God of."

נוּ   is the word ending (suffix) that means "us" or "our."

Write the English meaning of אֱלֹהֵינוּ. _____

Write the letters אֵל in the blanks to complete these words.

_____ _____   means "God."

הֵי _____ _____   means "God of."

הֵינוּ _____ _____   means "our God."

In the sentences below, draw a circle around every Hebrew word that includes the letters אֵל.

בָּרוּךְ אַתָּה יְיָ, אֱלֹהֵינוּ וֵאלֹהֵי אֲבוֹתֵינוּ, אֱלֹהֵי אַבְרָהָם,

אֱלֹהֵי יִצְחָק, וֵאלֹהֵי יַעֲקֹב. הָאֵל הַגָּדוֹל, הַגִּבּוֹר

וְהַנּוֹרָא, אֵל עֶלְיוֹן.

How many circles did you draw? _____

Read the circled words aloud.

אָבוֹת "ancestors"

אָב means "father" or "ancestor."

אָבוֹת means "fathers" or "ancestors."

The ending וּ means _____.

What does אֲבוֹתֵינוּ mean? _____

Draw a circle around the Hebrew names of the אָבוֹת.

בָּרוּךְ אַתָּה יְיָ, אֱלֹהֵינוּ וֵאלֹהֵי אֲבוֹתֵינוּ,

אֱלֹהֵי אַבְרָהָם, אֱלֹהֵי יִצְחָק, וֵאלֹהֵי יַעֲקֹב.

Why do you think the word אֱלֹהֵי ("God of") is repeated before the name of each אָב?

• • • • • • • • •

An Ethical Echo

זְכוּת אָבוֹת ("The Merit of the Ancestors")

An important theme of אָבוֹת is זְכוּת אָבוֹת, the "merit of the ancestors." The rabbis of long ago pointed to the connection between our ancestors — Abraham and Sarah, Isaac and Rebecca, Jacob and Leah and Rachel — and all the generations that came after them, including ours.

We have inherited a special "merit" from our ancestors because of *their* belief in God. Because of them, we have been favored with God's care and love.

A Point to Ponder

Is "the merit of the ancestors" enough for us to deserve God's care and love, or is there something we must do to earn it?

חֲסָדִים טוֹבִים "acts of lovingkindness"

חֲסָדִים   means "acts of lovingkindness."

טוֹבִים   means "good."

In the phrase חֲסָדִים טוֹבִים, the word טוֹבִים helps us know how *good* the acts of lovingkindness are.

Which of the following are חֲסָדִים טוֹבִים? Circle the numbers.

1   אַבְרָהָם welcomes and cares for strangers.
2   Haman forces the Jews to bow down to him.
3   You take home schoolwork to a sick friend.
4   A store owner gives employment to a needy person.

חַסְדֵי אָבוֹת "faithfulness of the ancestors"

חַסְדֵי   means "faithfulness of."

אָבוֹת   means "ancestors."

Circle the two Hebrew words that mean "faithfulness of the ancestors" in the part of the אָבוֹת prayer below.

גּוֹמֵל חֲסָדִים טוֹבִים, וְקוֹנֵה הַכֹּל,

וְזוֹכֵר חַסְדֵי אָבוֹת

Write the letters חסד below to complete the following words.

____ ____ ____ יִם   means "acts of lovingkindness."

____ ____ ____ י   means "faithfulness of."

In the Synagogue

אָבוֹת is the first blessing in a very old and very important prayer called the עֲמִידָה. The עֲמִידָה is the heart or center of every synagogue service.

The עֲמִידָה has many names:

- The Hebrew name עֲמִידָה means standing. We always stand when we say the עֲמִידָה. It is as if we are standing in front of יְיָ.

- It is sometimes called the Silent Prayer because many people say it in a very quiet voice. They are talking privately to יְיָ.

- Another name is שְׁמוֹנֶה עֶשְׂרֵה (the Hebrew word for eighteen). Originally, the עֲמִידָה contained eighteen blessings. Now it may have nineteen blessings (when it is said on a weekday) or seven blessings (when it is said on Shabbat and holidays). But many people still call this prayer the שְׁמוֹנֶה עֶשְׂרֵה.

- The עֲמִידָה is so important that it is sometimes simply called The Prayer (הַתְּפִלָּה).

● ● ● ● ● ● ● ● ●

True or False

Put a ✔ next to each sentence that is true.

___ אָבוֹת means "fathers" or "ancestors."

___ אָבוֹת is the last part of the עֲמִידָה.

___ The עֲמִידָה is said at every synagogue service.

___ Another name for the עֲמִידָה is שְׁמוֹנֶה עֶשְׂרֵה.

___ The עֲמִידָה always contains 18 blessings.

___ When we say "The Prayer," we are referring to the עֲמִידָה.

Fluent Reading

Each phrase contains a word you know. Practice reading the lines below.

• • • • • • • • •

1 אַבְרָהָם יָגֵל, יִצְחָק יְרַנֵּן, יַעֲקֹב וּבָנָיו יָנוּחוּ בוֹ.

2 בָּרוּךְ אַתָּה יְיָ אֱלֹהֵינוּ, מֶלֶךְ הָעוֹלָם, שֶׁעָשָׂה נִסִּים
   לַאֲבוֹתֵינוּ בַּיָּמִים הָהֵם בַּזְּמַן הַזֶּה.

3 מִי חָכָם וְיִשְׁמָר אֵלֶּה, וְיִתְבּוֹנְנוּ חַסְדֵי יְיָ.

4 וַיֹּאמַר, אֲנִי יְיָ, אֱלֹהֵי אַבְרָהָם אָבִיךָ, וֵאלֹהֵי יִצְחָק.

5 אֱלֹהֵינוּ וֵאלֹהֵי אֲבוֹתֵינוּ, זָכְרֵנוּ בְּזִכָּרוֹן טוֹב לְפָנֶיךָ.

6 רְצֵה יְיָ אֱלֹהֵינוּ בְּעַמְּךָ יִשְׂרָאֵל וּבִתְפִלָּתָם.

7 זָכְרָה לְחַסְדֵי דָּוִיד עַבְדֶּךָ.

8 בָּרוּךְ אַתָּה יְיָ, גּוֹמֵל חֲסָדִים טוֹבִים לְעַמּוֹ יִשְׂרָאֵל.

9 כְּמוֹ שֶׁנִּתְבָּרְכוּ אֲבוֹתֵינוּ אַבְרָהָם יִצְחָק וְיַעֲקֹב.

10 מְכַלְכֵּל חַיִּים בְּחֶסֶד, מְחַיֶּה הַכֹּל בְּרַחֲמִים רַבִּים.

2 אָבוֹת/אִמָּהוֹת

In the אָבוֹת we name many aspects of God's nature — a God who is mighty yet helps us, a God who is powerful yet protects us, a God who is awesome yet performs acts of lovingkindness.

• • • • • • • • •

Practice reading the אָבוֹת aloud.

1 בָּרוּךְ אַתָּה יְיָ, אֱלֹהֵינוּ וֵאלֹהֵי אֲבוֹתֵינוּ,

2 אֱלֹהֵי אַבְרָהָם, אֱלֹהֵי יִצְחָק, וֵאלֹהֵי יַעֲקֹב.

3 הָאֵל הַגָּדוֹל, הַגִּבּוֹר וְהַנּוֹרָא, אֵל עֶלְיוֹן.

4 גּוֹמֵל חֲסָדִים טוֹבִים, וְקוֹנֵה הַכֹּל, וְזוֹכֵר חַסְדֵי אָבוֹת,

5 וּמֵבִיא גְאֻלָּה (גוֹאֵל) לִבְנֵי בְנֵיהֶם, לְמַעַן שְׁמוֹ, בְּאַהֲבָה.

6 מֶלֶךְ עוֹזֵר וּמוֹשִׁיעַ וּמָגֵן.

7 בָּרוּךְ אַתָּה יְיָ, מָגֵן אַבְרָהָם.

Praised are You, Adonai, our God and God of our ancestors,
God of Abraham, God of Isaac, God of Jacob.
Great, mighty, and awesome God, supreme God.
God, to whom the world belongs, You do acts of lovingkindness
and recall the faithfulness of our ancestors.
You bring redemption (a redeemer) to their children's children for the sake of
Your name. God, You are our helper, and savior, and shield.
Praised are You, Adonai, the Shield of Abraham.

הָאֵל
the God

הַגָּדוֹל
the great

הַגִּבּוֹר
the mighty

וְהַנּוֹרָא
and the awesome

עֶלְיוֹן
supreme

מֶלֶךְ
ruler

עוֹזֵר
helper

וּמוֹשִׁיעַ
and savior

וּמָגֵן
and shield

God's Greatness

אָבוֹת lists four words to describe God's greatness. Write the English meaning for each one.

| ___ | ___ | ___ | ___ |

עֶלְיוֹן   וְהַנּוֹרָא   הַגִּבּוֹר   הַגָּדוֹל

In אָבוֹת we see four roles that God plays in the lives of the Jewish people.

Write the English meaning for each one.

| ___ | ___ | ___ | ___ |

וּמָגֵן   וּמוֹשִׁיעַ   עוֹזֵר   מֶלֶךְ

Match Game

Match the Hebrew word to its English meaning.

the God	הַגָּדוֹל
the great	הַגִּבּוֹר
and the awesome	וְהַנּוֹרָא
the mighty	עֶלְיוֹן
helper	מֶלֶךְ
supreme	הָאֵל
and shield	עוֹזֵר
and savior	וּמוֹשִׁיעַ
ruler	וּמָגֵן

13

Prayer Building Blocks

הָאֵל "the God"

....

הָאֵל is made up of two parts:

אֵל we know, means _____.

הָ at the beginning of a word means "the."

What does הָאֵל mean? _____

הַגָּדוֹל הַגִּבּוֹר וְהַנּוֹרָא "the great, the mighty, and the awesome"

....

הַגָּדוֹל means "the great."

הַגִּבּוֹר means "the mighty."

וְהַנּוֹרָא means "and the awesome."

Complete the following words describing God by adding the prefix "the."

נוֹרָא ____וְ גִּבּוֹר ____ גָּדוֹל ____ אֵל ____

Describing God

The אָבוֹת prayer describes God as

גָּדוֹל גִּבּוֹר נוֹרָא

1. Circle the word that means "awesome."
2. Underline the word that means "great."
3. Put a ✔ above the word that means "mighty."

Torah Connection

Read this verse from the Torah (Deuteronomy 10:17).

1 כִּי יְיָ אֱלֹהֵיכֶם הוּא אֱלֹהֵי הָאֱלֹהִים

2 וַאֲדֹנֵי הָאֲדֹנִים הָאֵל הַגָּדֹל הַגִּבֹּר וְהַנּוֹרָא

Do you recognize the underlined words?

Underline the same words as they appear in these Hebrew lines.

1 בָּרוּךְ אַתָּה יְיָ, אֱלֹהֵינוּ וֵאלֹהֵי אֲבוֹתֵינוּ,

2 אֱלֹהֵי אַבְרָהָם, אֱלֹהֵי יִצְחָק, וֵאלֹהֵי יַעֲקֹב.

3 הָאֵל הַגָּדוֹל, הַגִּבּוֹר וְהַנּוֹרָא, אֵל עֶלְיוֹן.

4 גּוֹמֵל חֲסָדִים טוֹבִים, וְקוֹנֵה הַכֹּל...

What is the name of this prayer? _____

Write the English meaning of the words you underlined.

_____

Why do you think the words הָאֵל הַגָּדוֹל הַגִּבּוֹר וְהַנּוֹרָא are written in the
Torah and repeated in the עֲמִידָה?

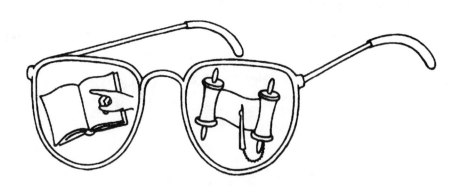

15

עֶלְיוֹן "supreme" or "highest"

עֶלְיוֹן means "supreme" or "highest."

The word עַל means "on" or "above."

Underline the Hebrew letters that mean "above" in this word.

עֶלְיוֹן

Why do you think God is called "supreme" or "highest"?

מֶלֶךְ עוֹזֵר וּמוֹשִׁיעַ וּמָגֵן "ruler, helper, and savior and shield"

מֶלֶךְ means "king, ruler."

עוֹזֵר means "helper."

וּמוֹשִׁיעַ means "and savior."

וּמָגֵן means "and shield."

Write the Hebrew word for "helper." _____

Write the Hebrew word for "and savior." _____

Circle the Hebrew word part that means "and" in these two words.

וּמוֹשִׁיעַ   וּמָגֵן

Fill in the Hebrew word for "shield" in the blanks.

מֶלֶךְ עוֹזֵר וּמוֹשִׁיעַ וּ_____ .

בָּרוּךְ אַתָּה יְיָ, _____ אַבְרָהָם.

Challenge Questions

1. Can you think of one example of God as the Savior of the Jewish people?

_____

_____

2. Why do you think God is compared to a shield?

_____

_____

3. Why do you think only Abraham is mentioned again at the end of אָבוֹת?

_____

_____

A Closer Look

אִמָהוֹת (Mothers of Israel)

Some synagogues include the names of the Mothers of Israel — Sarah, Rebecca, Leah, and Rachel — in the אָבוֹת. Practice reading the blessing.

1 בָּרוּךְ אַתָּה יְיָ, אֱלֹהֵינוּ וֵאלֹהֵי אֲבוֹתֵינוּ וְאִמוֹתֵינוּ,

2 אֱלֹהֵי אַבְרָהָם, אֱלֹהֵי יִצְחָק, וֵאלֹהֵי יַעֲקֹב, אֱלֹהֵי שָׂרָה,

3 אֱלֹהֵי רִבְקָה, אֱלֹהֵי לֵאָה וְרָחֵל, הָאֵל הַגָּדוֹל הַגִּבּוֹר

4 וְהַנּוֹרָא אֵל עֶלְיוֹן. גּוֹמֵל חֲסָדִים טוֹבִים וְקוֹנֵה הַכֹּל

5 וְזוֹכֵר חַסְדֵי אָבוֹת וְאִמָהוֹת וּמֵבִיא גְאֻלָה לִבְנֵי בְנֵיהֶם

6 לְמַעַן שְׁמוֹ בְּאַהֲבָה. מֶלֶךְ עוֹזֵר וּמוֹשִׁיעַ וּמָגֵן.

7 בָּרוּךְ אַתָּה יְיָ, מָגֵן אַבְרָהָם וְעֶזְרַת שָׂרָה.

Did you find the Hebrew names of the four Mothers of Israel in the prayer above? Underline the names and read them aloud.

Approaching God

Every service contains a version of the עֲמִידָה. The first three blessings and the last three blessings of every עֲמִידָה are always the same. Only the middle בְּרָכוֹת change. You have already learned the first blessing — אָבוֹת.

The first three and the last three blessings of the עֲמִידָה are nearly 2,500 years old! That goes back to the days of the Second Temple when the blessings were recited by the Kohanim (Priests) who worked there to serve God.

When we say the עֲמִידָה we approach God with our prayer. It is as if we are coming into the presence of a king or a queen, so we behave in a special way.

How do you think you would feel and behave in front of a king or a queen?

In some synagogues there is a series of actions we do when we say the עֲמִידָה.
1. We stand.
2. We face east, towards Jerusalem.
3. We take three small steps forward before we begin.
4. We bow at the beginning of אָבוֹת and at the end of אָבוֹת.
5. We bow several more times during the עֲמִידָה.
6. We don't stop to talk while reading the prayer.
7. We take three small steps backward when we finish the prayer.

Explain how these actions resemble a person's behavior when in the presence of a ruler.

_____

_____

Who is the Ruler we are addressing in the עֲמִידָה?

_____

Fluent Reading

Each phrase contains a word you know. Practice reading the lines below.

• • • • • • • • •

1   עֶזְרַת אֲבוֹתֵינוּ אַתָּה הוּא מֵעוֹלָם, מָגֵן וּמוֹשִׁיעַ.

2   אֱמֶת, אֱלֹהֵי עוֹלָם מַלְכֵּנוּ, צוּר יַעֲקֹב מָגֵן יִשְׁעֵנוּ.

3   אֶת שֵׁם הָאֵל הַמֶּלֶךְ הַגָּדוֹל, הַגִּבּוֹר וְהַנּוֹרָא, קָדוֹשׁ הוּא.

4   הָאֵל הַגָּדוֹל הַגִּבּוֹר, יְיָ צְבָאוֹת שְׁמוֹ.

5   כִּי בְשֵׁם קָדְשְׁךָ הַגָּדוֹל וְהַנּוֹרָא בָּטָחְנוּ.

6   מָגֵן אָבוֹת בִּדְבָרוֹ, מְחַיֵּה הַכֹּל בְּמַאֲמָרוֹ.

7   עַל הַתּוֹרָה וְעַל הָעֲבוֹדָה וְעַל גְּמִילוּת חֲסָדִים.

8   אָבִינוּ מַלְכֵּנוּ, עֲשֵׂה לְמַעַן שִׁמְךָ הַגָּדוֹל הַגִּבּוֹר וְהַנּוֹרָא.

9   עֹשֶׂה חֶסֶד לַאֲלָפִים.

10 לוּלֵי אֱלֹהֵי אָבִי, אֱלֹהֵי אַבְרָהָם, וּפַחַד יִצְחָק.

19

3 עֲשֶׂה שָׁלוֹם

Immediately after the עֲמִידָה we say the ancient prayer for peace —
עֲשֶׂה שָׁלוֹם. The quest for peace is as strong today as it has ever been for the
Jewish people.

• • • • • • • • •

Practice reading עֲשֶׂה שָׁלוֹם aloud.

1 עֲשֶׂה שָׁלוֹם בִּמְרוֹמָיו, הוּא יַעֲשֶׂה שָׁלוֹם עָלֵינוּ,

2 וְעַל כָּל־יִשְׂרָאֵל. וְאִמְרוּ, אָמֵן.

*God who makes peace in the heavens will make peace for us
and for all Israel. And say, Amen.*

One of the ways we seek to bring peace is through political demonstrations such as this one in
Washington D.C. These demonstrations help increase the awareness of the suffering and
oppression that people in other countries are often forced to endure.

PRAYER DICTIONARY

עֹשֶׂה
makes

שָׁלוֹם
peace

יַעֲשֶׂה
will make

עָלֵינוּ
for us, on us

וְעַל
and for, and on

כָּל
all

יִשְׂרָאֵל
Israel

וְאִמְרוּ
and say

אָמֵן
Amen

Note the Number

In the circle above each Hebrew word write the number of the correct English meaning.

◯   ◯   ◯

אָמֵן   יַעֲשֶׂה   שָׁלוֹם

◯   ◯   ◯

כָּל   וְאָמְרוּ   עָלֵינוּ

◯   ◯   ◯

יִשְׂרָאֵל   עֹשֶׂה   וְעַל

1 makes	2 and for	3 peace
4 Amen	5 Israel	6 will make
7 for us	8 all	9 and say

21

Family Words

There are two sets of family, or related, words in the list below.
They are:

I. makes   —   עֹשֶׂה   **II.** for us   —   עָלֵינוּ

    will make   —   יַעֲשֶׂה   and for   —   וְעַל

● ● ● ● ● ● ● ● ●

1. Draw a line between the family words.

עָלֵינוּ   עֹשֶׂה

יַעֲשֶׂה   וְעַל

2. Connect the word with its root.
Note: Sometimes a root letter is missing from the Hebrew word.

                                       עֹשֶׂה

(עשה)   עָלֵינוּ

(עלה)   וְעַל

                                       יַעֲשֶׂה

3. Write the root next to each word below.

I. עֹשֶׂה   ____ ____ ____

    יַעֲשֶׂה   ____ ____ ____

This root means *make*.

II. עָלֵינוּ   ____ ____ ____

    וְעַל   ____ ____ ____

This root means *on* or *for*.

4. Circle the three root letters in the following words.

לְמַעֲשֶׂה   וְעֹשֶׂה   שֶׁתַּעֲשֶׂה

Read the word כְּמַעֲשֶׂיךָ.

In this word you will find only two of the root letters.

What are they? _____ _____

Which root letter is missing? _____

All these Hebrew words have the root _____ _____ _____.

This root means _____.

5. Circle the root letters in the following words.
Remember: Sometimes a root letter is missing from a Hebrew word.

עֶלְיוֹן   עֲלִיָה   עָלֵינוּ   וְיִתְעַלֶה

Which root letter is missing in some of these words? _____

All these Hebrew words have the root _____ _____ _____.

This root means _____.

23

Did You Know?

In Hebrew we greet each other with the word שָׁלוֹם.

שָׁלוֹם   means "hello."

שָׁלוֹם   means "goodbye."

שָׁלוֹם   means "peace."

שָׁלוֹם comes from the Hebrew word שָׁלֵם, which means *complete* or *perfect*.

Why do you think the Hebrew word for *peace* also means *complete* or *perfect*?

● ● ● ● ● ● ● ● ●

According to legend, Jerusalem (יְרוּשָׁלַיִם), the capital city of Israel, is named for peace.

Find and circle the root letters that mean *peace* in the word

יְרוּשָׁלַיִם

King David was not allowed the honor of building the Holy Temple in יְרוּשָׁלַיִם because he was a man of war, a fighter. Instead, his son, שְׁלֹמֹה (Solomon), a peace-lover, built the Temple 3,000 years ago.

Find and circle the root letters that mean *peace* in King Solomon's name.

שְׁלֹמֹה

Reading Practice

Read the following excerpts aloud. Circle the word שָׁלוֹם in each sentence.

1 עוֹשֶׂה שָׁלוֹם וּבוֹרֵא אֶת הַכֹּל

2 שִׂים שָׁלוֹם טוֹבָה וּבְרָכָה חֵן וָחֶסֶד וְרַחֲמִים עָלֵינוּ

וְעַל כָּל יִשְׂרָאֵל עַמֶּךְ

3 בָּרוּךְ אַתָּה יְיָ הַמְבָרֵךְ אֶת עַמּוֹ יִשְׂרָאֵל בַּשָּׁלוֹם

4 וְאַהֲבַת חֶסֶד, וּצְדָקָה וּבְרָכָה וְרַחֲמִים וְחַיִּים וְשָׁלוֹם

5 מְנוּחַת שָׁלוֹם וְשַׁלְוָה וְהַשְׁקֵט וָבֶטַח

6 דְּרָכֶיהָ דַרְכֵי נֹעַם, וְכָל נְתִיבוֹתֶיהָ שָׁלוֹם

An Ethical Echo

Peace on earth begins with peace in our homes — within our families (שָׁלוֹם בַּיִת). Many of our mitzvot tell us how to behave towards our family members, for example, Honor your father and your mother.

A Point to Ponder

How can *you* contribute to peace within your family?

Why is peace within the home necessary before there can be peace among nations?

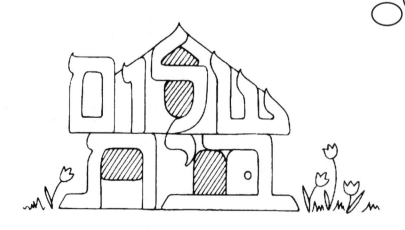

Prayer Building Blocks

עָלֵינוּ "for us"

....

עָלֵינוּ we know means "for us."

נוּ at the end of a word means _____.

We ask God to make peace for _____.

And for who else?

וְעַל כָּל יִשְׂרָאֵל and for all _____.

וְאִמְרוּ "and say"

....

וְאִמְרוּ   means "and say."

וְ   means _____.

אִמְרוּ   means _____.

The root letters of וְאִמְרוּ are אמר.
אמר tells us that *say* is part of a word's meaning.

Read the following sentences aloud. Circle the words with the root אמר.

1 וְאַל יֹאבַד יִשְׂרָאֵל, הָאוֹמְרִים "שְׁמַע יִשְׂרָאֵל"

2 וַיְהִי בִּנְסֹעַ הָאָרֹן וַיֹּאמֶר מֹשֶׁה

3 בָּרוּךְ שֶׁאָמַר וְהָיָה הָעוֹלָם, בָּרוּךְ הוּא

4 בָּרוּךְ אוֹמֵר וְעוֹשֶׂה

5 וּבְדִבְרֵי קָדְשְׁךָ כָּתוּב לֵאמֹר

Write the root of the circled words. _____ _____ _____

This root means _____.

From the Tanach

The quest for peace, for שָׁלוֹם, has always been important to the Jewish people. Read this verse from the prophet Isaiah and answer the questions that follow.

> *And they shall beat their swords into plowshares*
> *And their spears into pruning-hooks;*
> *Nation shall not lift up sword against nation,*
> *Neither shall they learn war any more.*

(Isaiah 2:4)

1. Isaiah lived more than 2,500 years ago. Why are his words still important today?

_____

_____

2. List the words in the verse that are the opposite of peace.

_____

_____

3. In one sentence describe Isaiah's ideal world.

_____

_____

A Closer Look

עֹשֶׂה שָׁלוֹם is said after the conclusion of the עֲמִידָה in some services. It also appears as part of two other prayers, Grace After Meals (בִּרְכַּת הַמָּזוֹן) and the Kaddish. When we say עֹשֶׂה שָׁלוֹם at the end of the Kaddish, it is traditional to take three steps backward and to turn to the left and to the right, as if the person who is praying is leaving God — the Ruler's — presence.

• • • • • • • • •

Here is a section of בִּרְכַּת הַמָּזוֹן. Find and underline the עֹשֶׂה שָׁלוֹם prayer.

1 הָרַחֲמָן, הוּא יְזַכֵּנוּ לִימוֹת הַמָּשִׁיחַ, וּלְחַיֵּי הָעוֹלָם הַבָּא:

2 מִגְדּוֹל יְשׁוּעוֹת מַלְכּוֹ, וְעֹשֶׂה־חֶסֶד לִמְשִׁיחוֹ,

3 לְדָוִד וּלְזַרְעוֹ עַד־עוֹלָם. עֹשֶׂה שָׁלוֹם בִּמְרוֹמָיו,

4 הוּא יַעֲשֶׂה שָׁלוֹם עָלֵינוּ, וְעַל־כָּל־יִשְׂרָאֵל. וְאִמְרוּ אָמֵן:

Fluent Reading

Each phrase contains a word you know. Practice reading the lines below.

• • • • • • • • •

1. הַפּוֹרֵשׂ סֻכַּת שָׁלוֹם עָלֵינוּ , וְעַל כָּל עַמּוֹ יִשְׂרָאֵל,
וְעַל יְרוּשָׁלָיִם.

2. שָׁלוֹם רָב עַל יִשְׂרָאֵל עַמְּךָ תָּשִׂים לְעוֹלָם.

3. כִּי אַתָּה הוּא מֶלֶךְ אָדוֹן לְכָל הַשָּׁלוֹם.

4. בָּרוּךְ אַתָּה יְיָ, הַמְבָרֵךְ אֶת עַמּוֹ יִשְׂרָאֵל בַּשָּׁלוֹם.

5. רַחֵם, יְיָ אֱלֹהֵינוּ, עַל יִשְׂרָאֵל עַמְּךָ, וְעַל יְרוּשָׁלַיִם עִירֶךָ.

6. שָׁלוֹם עֲלֵיכֶם, מַלְאֲכֵי הַשָּׁרֵת, מַלְאֲכֵי עֶלְיוֹן.

7. שִׂים שָׁלוֹם, טוֹבָה וּבְרָכָה, חֵן וָחֶסֶד וְרַחֲמִים עָלֵינוּ
וְעַל כָּל יִשְׂרָאֵל עַמֶּךָ.

8. בָּרוּךְ אַתָּה, יְיָ אֱלֹהֵינוּ, מֶלֶךְ הָעוֹלָם, יוֹצֵר אוֹר
וּבוֹרֵא חֹשֶׁךְ עֹשֶׂה שָׁלוֹם וּבוֹרֵא אֶת הַכֹּל.

4

כִּי מִצִּיּוֹן; לְךָ יְיָ

The Torah service is divided into 3 parts:

1. Taking the Torah from the Ark.
2. Reading the Torah.
3. Returning the Torah to the Ark.

In this lesson we will learn about:

Taking the Torah from the Ark סֵדֶר הוֹצָאַת הַתּוֹרָה

The Torah reading is the climax of the Shabbat morning service. We honor the Torah with special blessings, songs, and a procession. This is a time for us to show how much we love and respect the Torah. It is also a time to honor people from the congregation by calling them up to recite the Torah blessings.

● ● ● ● ● ● ● ● ●

The Holy Ark is open, everyone in the synagogue is standing, and the Torah is taken out of the Ark as we sing these words:

1 כִּי מִצִּיּוֹן תֵּצֵא תוֹרָה, וּדְבַר־יְיָ מִירוּשָׁלָיִם.

For out of Zion shall go forth Torah, and the word of God from Jerusalem.

2 בָּרוּךְ שֶׁנָּתַן תּוֹרָה לְעַמּוֹ יִשְׂרָאֵל בִּקְדֻשָּׁתוֹ.

Praised be the One, who in holiness gave the Torah to the people Israel.

מִצִּיּוֹן

from Zion

תּוֹרָה

Torah, teaching

וּדְבַר

and the word of

מִירוּשָׁלַיִם

from Jerusalem

שֶׁנָּתַן

who gave

לְעַמּוֹ

to God's people

בִּקְדֻשָּׁתוֹ

in God's holiness

True or False

Put a ✔ next to each sentence that is true.

____ The Torah service is the climax of the Shabbat morning service.

____ The Torah service is divided into 4 parts.

____ We remain seated as the Torah is taken from the Ark.

____ The Torah service concludes with the reading from the Torah.

Match Game

Connect the Hebrew word to its English meaning.

to God's people   תּוֹרָה

from Zion   וּדְבַר

and the word of   מִירוּשָׁלַיִם

from Jerusalem   מִצִּיּוֹן

in God's holiness   שֶׁנָּתַן

who gave   לְעַמּוֹ

Torah, teaching   בִּקְדֻשָּׁתוֹ

Torah Reading

How did the custom of reading the Torah originate?

In about the year 400 B.C.E. (that's nearly 2,500 years ago!), many Jews who had been in exile in Babylon were allowed to return to the Land of Israel. But by then they had forgotten the teachings of the Torah.

Determined to rebuild Jewish life in Israel, Ezra the Scribe stood during Rosh Hashanah in front of the gathered Jews and read to them from the Torah. The Jews cried when they heard the words of the Torah again.

They returned the second day of Rosh Hashanah to study Torah with Ezra, and they celebrated Sukkot for the first time in many years. But Ezra knew that they would have to be reminded of the contents of the Torah if they were to live according to its laws. So Ezra arranged public Torah readings on Mondays and Thursdays, on Shabbat, and on certain holidays.

Why on Mondays and Thursdays?
Those were market days when the people came together in large numbers to do business.

And to this day — thousands of years later — many congregations still read from the Torah in the synagogue on Monday and Thursday, on Shabbat, and on certain holidays.

● ● ● ● ● ● ● ● ●

How did reading from the Torah out loud and in public help the Jews in Ezra's time?

Why do you think it is important to continue this tradition?

What's Missing?

Circle the word that completes each sentence.

1 כִּי _____ תֵּצֵא תוֹרָה | מִצִּיּוֹן מִירוּשָׁלַיְם לְעַמּוֹ

from Zion

2 וּדְבַר יְיָ _____ | תוֹרָה מִירוּשָׁלַיְם מִצִּיּוֹן

from Jerusalem

3 בָּרוּךְ שֶׁנָּתַן _____ | יְיָ יִשְׂרָאֵל תוֹרָה

Torah

4 לְעַמּוֹ _____ בִּקְדֻשָּׁתוֹ | יִשְׂרָאֵל מִצִּיּוֹן וּדְבַר

Israel

Out of Order

I. Number the *seven* words from the first line of כִּי מִצִּיּוֹן in the correct order.

תוֹרָה ◯   וּדְבַר ◯   תֵּצֵא ◯

מִירוּשָׁלַיְם ◯   מִצִּיּוֹן ◯

כִּי ◯   יְיָ ◯

II. Number the *six* words from the second line of כִּי מִצִּיּוֹן in the correct order.

לְעַמּוֹ ◯   יִשְׂרָאֵל ◯

בָּרוּךְ ◯   שֶׁנָּתַן ◯

בִּקְדֻשָּׁתוֹ ◯   תוֹרָה ◯

Prayer Building Blocks

מִצִּיּוֹן "from Zion"

מִצִּיּוֹן is made up of two parts.

    מִ   is a prefix meaning "from."

    צִיּוֹן   means "Zion."

    מִצִּיּוֹן   means _____.

Zion is another name for *Jerusalem*.

Underline the Hebrew word for *Zion* in the last lines of the Israeli national anthem, *Hatikvah (The Hope)*.

הַתִּקְוָה בַּת שְׁנוֹת אַלְפַּיִם

לִהְיוֹת עַם חָפְשִׁי בְּאַרְצֵנוּ,

אֶרֶץ צִיּוֹן וִירוּשָׁלָיִם.

תּוֹרָה "teaching"

תּוֹרָה comes from the root meaning *to teach* or *to shoot*.

מוֹרֶה and מוֹרָה (teacher) come from the same root.

תּוֹרָה is more than the contents of a Torah scroll; it includes *all Jewish studies*.

תּוֹרָה comes from the root meaning _____ or _____.

וּדְבַר "and the word of"

וּ is a prefix meaning _____.

דְּבַר means "the word of."

Read the following sentences and circle all the words that come from the root
דבר (word or thing).

1 וְהָיוּ הַדְּבָרִים הָאֵלֶּה, אֲשֶׁר אָנֹכִי מְצַוְּךָ הַיּוֹם, עַל לְבָבֶךָ.

2 בָּרוּךְ אַתָּה יְיָ, הָאֵל הַנֶּאֱמָן בְּכָל דְּבָרָיו.

3 וְעֵינֵינוּ תִרְאֶינָה מַלְכוּתֶךָ כַּדָּבָר הָאָמוּר בְּשִׁירֵי עֻזֶּךָ.

4 וְדָבָר אֶחָד מִדְּבָרֶיךָ אָחוֹר לֹא יָשׁוּב רֵיקָם.

5 הָאֵל הַנֶּאֱמָן, הָאוֹמֵר וְעוֹשֶׂה, הַמְדַבֵּר וּמְקַיֵּם.

מִירוּשָׁלָיִם "from Jerusalem"

מִירוּשָׁלָיִם is made up of two parts.

מִ is a prefix meaning "from."

יְרוּשָׁלַיִם we know, means "Jerusalem."

The prophet Isaiah first said the words:

כִּי מִצִּיּוֹן תֵּצֵא תוֹרָה, וּדְבַר־יְיָ מִירוּשָׁלָיִם.

They later became part of the Torah service.

Complete the prayer by filling in the blanks with the correct English word.

For out of _____ will go forth _____ , and the word of

צִיּוֹן   תּוֹרָה

_____ _____ .

מִירוּשָׁלָיִם   יְיָ

35

Read these sentences and underline the Hebrew word for *Jerusalem* in each one.

1 וּבְנֵה יְרוּשָׁלַיִם עִיר הַקֹּדֶשׁ בִּמְהֵרָה בְיָמֵינוּ.

2 אַב הָרַחֲמִים, הֵיטִיבָה בִרְצוֹנְךָ אֶת צִיּוֹן,
   תִּבְנֶה חוֹמוֹת יְרוּשָׁלָיִם.

3 תִּתְגַּדַּל וְתִתְקַדַּשׁ בְּתוֹךְ יְרוּשָׁלַיִם עִירְךָ.

4 בָּרוּךְ אַתָּה יְיָ, בּוֹנֵה בְרַחֲמָיו יְרוּשָׁלָיִם, אָמֵן.

5 שִׂמְחוּ אֶת יְרוּשָׁלַיִם וְגִילוּ בָהּ כָּל אֹהֲבֶיהָ.

• • • • • • • • •

שֶׁנָּתַן "who gave"

....

שֶׁנָּתַן   is made up of two parts.

שֶׁ   is a prefix meaning "who."

נָתַן   means "gave."

בָּרוּךְ שֶׁנָּתַן תּוֹרָה means *Praised is the One who gave the Torah.*

Who is the One who gave us the Torah?

Write your answer in Hebrew._____

לְעַמּוֹ "to God's people"

....

לְ   is a prefix meaning "to."

עַמּוֹ   means "God's people."

עַם   means "people" or "nation."

וֹ   at the end of a word means "his."

As God is neither male nor female, we translate the word לְעַמּוֹ as "to God's people."

36

בְּ   is a prefix meaning "in."

קָדְשָׁה   means "holiness."

קָדְשָׁתוֹ   means "God's holiness."

בְּקָדְשָׁתוֹ   means _____.

What is the root of בְּקָדְשָׁתוֹ? _____ _____ _____

This root means *holy.*

Circle the three root letters for *holy* in each word:

קָדְשְׁךָ   מַקְדִּישִׁים   הַקָּדוֹשׁ   וַיְקַדֵּשׁ

וּקְדוֹשִׁים   קָדוֹשׁ

• • • • • • • • •

Prefixes

Circle the prefixes in the following words.
Write the prefixes next to their English meaning below.

שֶׁנָּתַן   מִצִּיּוֹן   וְדָבָר   מִירוּשָׁלָיִם

לְעַמּוֹ   בְּקָדְשָׁתוֹ

who _____   from _____   and _____

to _____   in _____

Words of Praise

We sing the following words as the Torah is carried from the Ark to the reading stand. Often the congregants touch the Torah with their tallit or siddur, which they then kiss. We respect the Torah so much that we do not reach out to touch it with our bare hands.

Practice reading the prayer below.

1   לְךָ, יְיָ, הַגְּדֻלָּה וְהַגְּבוּרָה וְהַתִּפְאֶרֶת וְהַנֵּצַח וְהַהוֹד,

2   כִּי כֹל בַּשָּׁמַיִם וּבָאָרֶץ, לְךָ יְיָ הַמַּמְלָכָה
וְהַמִּתְנַשֵּׂא לְכֹל לְרֹאשׁ.

Yours, God, is the greatness, the power, the glory, the victory, and the majesty;
for all that is in heaven and earth is Yours. Yours is the kingdom, God;
You are supreme over all.

Look again at the prayer above.

Notice that no mention is made of the Torah in this prayer.
You might expect us to say special words about the Torah as we carry it lovingly from the Ark, but instead we praise God.

Why do we praise God instead of the Torah?
Because, although we honor the Torah and respect it, *we worship only God.*

Why do you think this prayer encourages us to worship God and not the Torah?

Fluent Reading

Each phrase contains a word you know. Practice reading the lines below.

● ● ● ● ● ● ● ● ●

1 בָּרוּךְ אַתָּה יְיָ הָאֵל הַנֶּאֱמָן בְּכָל דְּבָרָיו.

2 אוֹר חָדָשׁ עַל צִיּוֹן תָּאִיר וְנִזְכֶּה כֻלָּנוּ מְהֵרָה לְאוֹרוֹ.

3 וּבְדִבְרֵי קָדְשְׁךָ כָּתוּב לֵאמֹר: יִמְלֹךְ יְיָ לְעוֹלָם אֱלֹהַיִךְ
צִיּוֹן לְדֹר וָדֹר הַלְלוּיָהּ.

4 אִם אֶשְׁכָּחֵךְ יְרוּשָׁלַיִם תִּשְׁכַּח יְמִינִי.

5 גָּדוֹל יְיָ וּמְהֻלָּל מְאֹד וְלִגְדֻלָּתוֹ אֵין חֵקֶר.

6 כִּי בָנוּ בָחַרְתָּ וְאוֹתָנוּ קִדַּשְׁתָּ.

7 רְצֵה יְיָ אֱלֹהֵינוּ בְּעַמְּךָ יִשְׂרָאֵל וּבִתְפִלָּתָם.

8 הָאֵל הַגָּדוֹל הַגִּבּוֹר וְהַנּוֹרָא, אֵל עֶלְיוֹן.

9 בָּרוּךְ אַתָּה, יְיָ, הַבּוֹחֵר בַּתּוֹרָה, וּבְמֹשֶׁה עַבְדּוֹ,
וּבְיִשְׂרָאֵל עַמּוֹ, וּבִנְבִיאֵי הָאֱמֶת וָצֶדֶק.

בִּרְכוֹת הַתּוֹרָה

The Torah lies open on the reader's stand. It's time for the Reading From the Torah — קְרִיאַת הַתּוֹרָה.

It is a great honor to be called up to read from the Torah.

Below is the blessing we say *before* the Torah reading begins.

• • • • • • • • •

Blessing Before the Torah Reading

Practice reading the blessing.

1   בָּרְכוּ אֶת־יְיָ הַמְבֹרָךְ.

2   בָּרוּךְ יְיָ הַמְבֹרָךְ לְעוֹלָם וָעֶד.

3   בָּרוּךְ אַתָּה, יְיָ אֱלֹהֵינוּ, מֶלֶךְ הָעוֹלָם,

4   אֲשֶׁר בָּחַר־בָּנוּ מִכָּל־הָעַמִּים,

5   וְנָתַן־לָנוּ אֶת־תּוֹרָתוֹ.

6   בָּרוּךְ אַתָּה, יְיָ, נוֹתֵן הַתּוֹרָה.

Praise Adonai, who is praised.

Praised is Adonai, who is praised forever and ever.

Praised are You, Adonai our God, Ruler of the world,

who chose us from all the nations

and gave us the Torah.

Praised are You, Adonai, who gives us the Torah.

Match Game

Connect the Hebrew word to its English meaning.

us	בָּחַר
and gave	בָּנוּ
chose	מִכָּל הָעַמִּים
to us	וְנָתַן
God's Torah	נוֹתֵן
gives	לָנוּ
from all the nations	תּוֹרָתוֹ

בָּחַר
chose

בָּנוּ
us

מִכָּל
from all

הָעַמִּים
the nations

וְנָתַן
and gave

לָנוּ
to us

תּוֹרָתוֹ
God's Torah

נוֹתֵן
gives

41

Crossword

Read the Hebrew clues and fill in the missing English words.

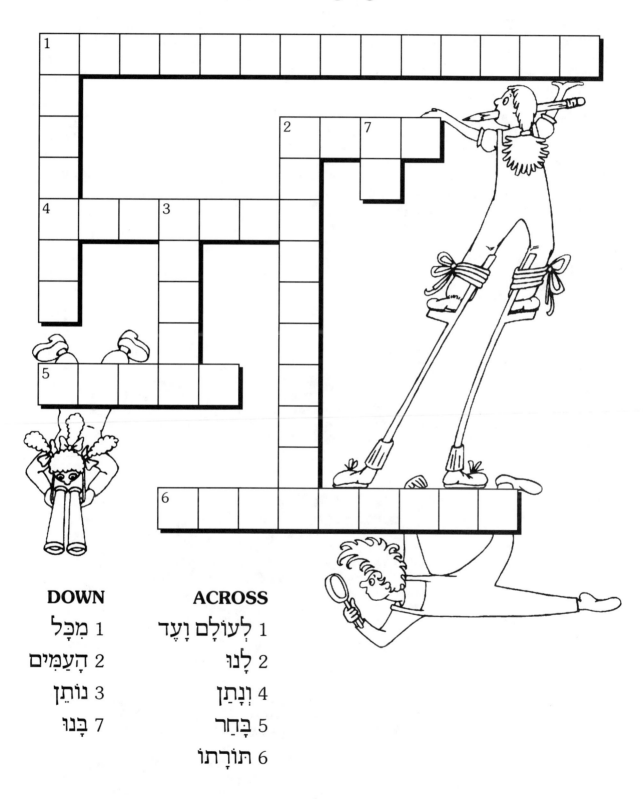

DOWN

1 מִכָּל

2 הָעַמִּים

3 נוֹתֵן

7 בָּנוּ

ACROSS

1 לְעוֹלָם וָעֶד

2 לָנוּ

4 וְנָתַן

5 בָּחַר

6 תּוֹרָתוֹ

Letter Link

It is no easy task to read from the Torah. You must be trained to read Hebrew fluently, and without vowels, in order to understand the words and to read without mistakes. What's more, in many synagogues the Torah portion is chanted using special melodies called *trope*.

An expert trained in Torah reading, called a בַּעַל קְרִיאָה (masculine), בַּעֲלַת קְרִיאָה (feminine), reads the words of the Torah, and the congregant honored with an עֲלִיָּה (being called up to the Torah) recites the blessings before and after the Torah reading.

Here is the way Hebrew letters look in a Torah scroll.

אבגדהוזחטיכרלמסנסעפפצץקרשת

• • • • • • • • •

Connect each Torah letter to the matching printed letter.

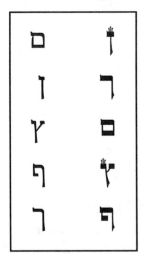

Prayer Building Blocks

Read the first lines of the Torah blessing. Do you recognize these two lines?

1 ‏בָּרְכוּ אֶת־יְיָ הַמְבֹרָךְ.

2 ‏בָּרוּךְ יְיָ הַמְבֹרָךְ לְעוֹלָם וָעֶד.

The Torah reading begins with the ‏בָּרְכוּ‎ — *the call to worship*, the official opening of the prayer service.

Circle all the words in the ‏בָּרְכוּ‎ that are built on the ‏שֹׁרֶשׁ‎ (root) ‏ברכ‎.

This root means _____.

Now read the next part of the Torah blessing.

1 ‏בָּרוּךְ אַתָּה, יְיָ אֱלֹהֵינוּ, מֶלֶךְ הָעוֹלָם,

2 ‏אֲשֶׁר בָּחַר־בָּנוּ מִכָּל־הָעַמִּים, וְנָתַן־לָנוּ אֶת־תּוֹרָתוֹ.

Underline the 6 words that are found at the beginning of most ‏בְּרָכוֹת‎.

‏אֲשֶׁר בָּחַר בָּנוּ‎ "who chose us"

‏אֲשֶׁר‎   means "who."

‏בָּחַר‎   means "chose."

‏בָּנוּ‎   means "us."

Who is the One who chose us? _____

To whom does "us" refer? _____

44

וְנָתַן לָנוּ אֶת תּוֹרָתוֹ "and gave us God's Torah"

וְנָתַן means "and gave."

וְ we know, is a prefix meaning _____.

נָתַן means _____.

לָנוּ means "to us."

תּוֹרָתוֹ is made up of two word parts: תּוֹרָה and the word ending וֹ (his).

Because God is neither male nor female, we translate תּוֹרָתוֹ as *God's Torah*.

What did God give us? _____

Now write your answer in Hebrew. _____

Facts and Figures About the Torah Reading

- The Torah (also called the Five Books of Moses or the חֻמָּשׁ) is divided into 54 portions.

- It takes exactly one year to read the whole Torah. We begin reading the first book, Genesis (בְּרֵאשִׁית), on Simḥat Torah, and read the last word of the last book, Deuteronomy (דְּבָרִים), one year later on the next Simḥat Torah.

- Each Torah portion is divided into smaller readings called עֲלִיּוֹת (singular: עֲלִיָּה).

- The last person called to the Torah on Shabbat is known as the *maftir*. This is often the bar mitzvah boy or bat mitzvah girl, who is honored with this special עֲלִיָּה. The maftir reads the last עֲלִיָּה and then chants a portion from Prophets called the *haftarah*.

1. How many portions are contained in the Torah?

   _____

2. On what holiday do we finish reading the Torah and begin all over again?

   _____

3. Explain in your own words what the *maftir* does.

   _____

   _____

46

Aliyah

The honor of being called up from the congregation to read from the Torah is known as an עֲלִיָּה. עֲלִיָּה is translated as "going up." We *go up* to the bimah when called to read from the Torah. You may have heard the word עֲלִיָּה in a different context. Going to live in Israel is also called עֲלִיָּה. We don't just *move* to the Holy Land, we *ascend*, or *go up* to it.

Circle the common letters in each of these words.

עָלֵינוּ   עֶלְיוֹן   עַל   עֲלִיָּה

All these words have to do with _____.

Blessing After the Torah Reading

When the עֲלִיָּה is over, the person called to read from the Torah says a special blessing.

Practice reading the blessing said on completion of the Torah reading.

1   בָּרוּךְ אַתָּה, יְיָ אֱלֹהֵינוּ, מֶלֶךְ הָעוֹלָם,

2   אֲשֶׁר נָתַן־לָנוּ תּוֹרַת אֱמֶת

3   וְחַיֵּי עוֹלָם נָטַע בְּתוֹכֵנוּ.

4   בָּרוּךְ אַתָּה, יְיָ, נוֹתֵן הַתּוֹרָה.

Praised are You, Adonai our God, Ruler of the world,
who gave us the Torah of truth,
and implanted within us eternal life.
Praised are You, Adonai, who gives us the Torah.

Underline all the words that indicate this is a blessing.

Phrase Match

Connect the Hebrew phrase to its English meaning.

and eternal life   לְעוֹלָם וָעֶד

ruler of the world   תּוֹרַת אֱמֶת

forever and ever   וְחַיֵּי עוֹלָם

Torah of truth   מֶלֶךְ הָעוֹלָם

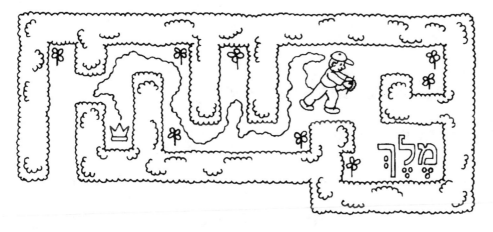

What's Missing?

Fill in the missing Hebrew words in the prayer.

בָּרוּךְ אַתָּה, יְיָ אֱלֹהֵינוּ, מֶלֶךְ הָעוֹלָם,

אֲשֶׁר נָתַן־לָנוּ _____ _____
                Torah of truth

נָטַע בְּתוֹכֵנוּ. _____ _____
               and eternal life

בָּרוּךְ אַתָּה, יְיָ, _____ הַתּוֹרָה.
                 gives

PRAYER DICTIONARY

תּוֹרַת
Torah of

_____

אֱמֶת
truth

_____

וְחַיֵּי
and life

_____

עוֹלָם
eternal, world

Prayer Building Blocks

אֲשֶׁר נָתַן לָנוּ תּוֹרַת אֱמֶת "who gave us the Torah of truth"

....

נָתַן לָנוּ   we know, means _____.

תּוֹרַת אֱמֶת   means "Torah of truth."

תּוֹרַת   is a combination word that means "Torah of."

אֱמֶת   means "truth."

Fill in the missing phrase _____ אֲשֶׁר נָתַן לָנוּ

What did God give us? _____

וְחַיֵּי עוֹלָם "and eternal life"

....

וְחַיֵּי   means "and a life of."

וְ   is a prefix meaning _____.

חַיֵּי   means "a life of."

The word for *life* is חַיִּים. (Do you know the toast "!לְחַיִּים" — "To life!"?)

עוֹלָם   means "eternal."

עוֹלָם   also means "world."

וְחַיֵּי עוֹלָם   means _____.

49

Read the following sentences and underline עוֹלָם in each one.

1 וְשִׁבְחֲךָ אֱלֹהֵינוּ מִפִּינוּ לֹא יָמוּשׁ לְעוֹלָם וָעֶד.

2 אֲדוֹן עוֹלָם אֲשֶׁר מָלַךְ בְּטֶרֶם כָּל יְצִיר נִבְרָא.

3 יִתְבָּרַךְ שִׁמְךָ בְּפִי כָל חַי תָּמִיד לְעוֹלָם וָעֶד.

4 וַאֲנַחְנוּ נְבָרֵךְ יָהּ מֵעַתָּה וְעַד עוֹלָם.

5 נְקַדֵּשׁ אֶת שִׁמְךָ בָּעוֹלָם, כְּשֵׁם שֶׁמַּקְדִּישִׁים אוֹתוֹ בִּשְׁמֵי מָרוֹם.

6 אֵל חַי וְקַיָּם תָּמִיד יִמְלֹךְ עָלֵינוּ לְעוֹלָם וָעֶד.

Challenge Question

Reread the blessing after the Torah reading.

In your own words, describe the theme, or main idea, of this blessing.

_____

_____

_____

50

Fluent Reading

Each phrase contains a word you know. Practice reading the lines below.

• • • • • • • • •

1 בָּרוּךְ שֶׁנָּתַן תּוֹרָה לְעַמּוֹ יִשְׂרָאֵל בִּקְדֻשָּׁתוֹ.

2 יְהִי שֵׁם יְיָ מְבֹרָךְ, מֵעַתָּה וְעַד עוֹלָם.

3 הוּא נוֹתֵן לֶחֶם לְכָל בָּשָׂר.

4 תּוֹרָה וּמִצְוֹת, חֻקִּים וּמִשְׁפָּטִים אוֹתָנוּ לִמַּדְתָּ.

5 שֶׁכָּל דְּבָרָיו אֱמֶת וָצֶדֶק.

6 וְתִתֶּן לָנוּ חַיִּים אֲרֻכִּים, חַיִּים שֶׁל שָׁלוֹם,
חַיִּים שֶׁל טוֹבָה, חַיִּים שֶׁל בְּרָכָה.

7 כַּכָּתוּב בְּתוֹרָתֶךָ: יְיָ יִמְלֹךְ לְעֹלָם וָעֶד.

8 אֵין לָנוּ מֶלֶךְ אֶלָּא אָתָּה.

9 חַיִּים שֶׁתְּהֵי בָנוּ אַהֲבַת תּוֹרָה וְיִרְאַת שָׁמַיִם.

10 כִּי אַתָּה שׁוֹמֵעַ תְּפִלַּת עַמְּךָ יִשְׂרָאֵל.

11 לְחַיִּים וּלְשָׁלוֹם, לְשָׂשׂוֹן וּלְשִׂמְחָה, לִישׁוּעָה וּלְנֶחָמָה,
וְנֹאמַר אָמֵן.

51

6 וְזֹאת הַתּוֹרָה; עֵץ חַיִּים הִיא; עַל שְׁלֹשָׁה דְבָרִים

It is time to return the Torah to the Ark — סֵדֶר הַכְנָסַת הַתּוֹרָה.
After the Torah reading, the Torah is lifted up high for all the congregation to see.
The honor of lifting the Torah is known as הַגְבָּהָה. All eyes are on the Torah as
worshippers stand and chant this prayer, וְזֹאת הַתּוֹרָה.

• • • • • • • • •

Practice reading וְזֹאת הַתּוֹרָה aloud.

1 וְזֹאת הַתּוֹרָה אֲשֶׁר־שָׂם מֹשֶׁה לִפְנֵי בְּנֵי יִשְׂרָאֵל,

2 עַל־פִּי יְיָ בְּיַד־מֹשֶׁה.

And this is the Torah that Moses placed before the people of Israel
to fulfill the word of God through Moses.

52

Search and Circle

Circle the Hebrew word that means the same as the English.

English			
and this is	וְחַיֵּי עוֹלָם	וְזֹאת	וְנָתַן
put, placed	שָׁם	בָּחַר	עוֹשֶׂה
Moses	מֹשֶׁה	מֶלֶךְ	מִצִּיּוֹן
before	לָנוּ	לְפְנֵי	בָּנוּ
Israel	אֲבוֹתֵינוּ	לְעוֹלָם וָעֶד	יִשְׂרָאֵל

Prayer Dictionary (sidebar)

וְזֹאת
and this is

שָׁם
placed, put

מֹשֶׁה
Moses

לְפְנֵי
before

בְּנֵי
people of

יִשְׂרָאֵל
Israel

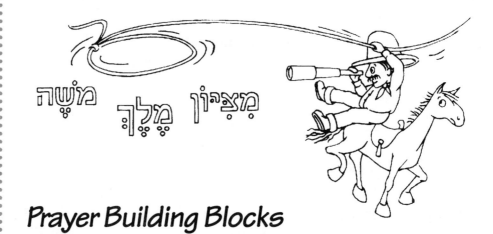

Prayer Building Blocks

וְזֹאת הַתּוֹרָה "and this is the Torah"

וְזֹאת	means "and this is."
וְ	means _____.
זֹאת	means _____.
הַ	means _____.
וְזֹאת הַתּוֹרָה	means _____.

From the Sources

The prayer וְזֹאת הַתּוֹרָה is taken from two verses in the Torah.

Below are three verses from the Torah. Find and underline all the words of וְזֹאת הַתּוֹרָה. (Remember: יְיָ can also be written יְהֹוָה.) Practice reading these Biblical verses.

44 בַּבָּשָׁן לַמְנַשִּׁי: וְזֹאת הַתּוֹרָה אֲשֶׁר־שָׂם

45 מֹשֶׁה לִפְנֵי בְּנֵי יִשְׂרָאֵל: אֵלֶּה הָעֵדֹת

וְהַחֻקִּים וְהַמִּשְׁפָּטִים אֲשֶׁר דִּבֶּר מֹשֶׁה

אֶל־בְּנֵי יִשְׂרָאֵל בְּצֵאתָם מִמִּצְרָיִם: (דברים 4)

23 מִשְׁמֶרֶת יְהֹוָה שָׁמָרוּ עַל־פִּי יְהֹוָה בְּיַד־מֹשֶׁה: (במדבר 9)

אֲשֶׁר שָׂם מֹשֶׁה "that Moses placed"

שָׂם   means "put" or "placed."

מֹשֶׁה   we know, means "Moses."

What did Moses place? Write your answer in Hebrew. _____

Read these sentences aloud and underline the Hebrew word for Moses in each one.

1 וַיְהִי בִּנְסֹעַ הָאָרֹן וַיֹּאמֶר מֹשֶׁה

2 לֹא קָם בְּיִשְׂרָאֵל כְּמֹשֶׁה עוֹד נָבִיא, וּמַבִּיט אֶת תְּמוּנָתוֹ

3 בָּרוּךְ אַתָּה יְיָ, הַבּוֹחֵר בַּתּוֹרָה וּבְמֹשֶׁה עַבְדוֹ...

וּבְנְבִיאֵי הָאֱמֶת וָצֶדֶק

4 תּוֹרָה צִוָּה לָנוּ מֹשֶׁה, מוֹרָשָׁה קְהִלַּת יַעֲקֹב

לִפְנֵי בְּנֵי יִשְׂרָאֵל "before the people of Israel"

לִפְנֵי means "before."

בְּנֵי יִשְׂרָאֵל means "the people of Israel."

Examine the underlined part of this prayer:

וְזֹאת הַתּוֹרָה אֲשֶׁר־שָׂם מֹשֶׁה לִפְנֵי בְּנֵי יִשְׂרָאֵל,

עַל־פִּי יְיָ בְּיַד־מֹשֶׁה.

These words are translated as *to fulfill the word of God through Moses.*

- Circle the Hebrew word for God in the underlined part of the Hebrew prayer.

- Put a star above the Hebrew word for Moses.

- Whose words or mitzvot are contained in the Torah?

  Write your answer in Hebrew. _____

- Who brought those words or mitzvot to the people?

  Write your answer in Hebrew. _____

עֵץ חַיִּים הִיא

The Torah is rolled and closed in a ceremony called גְּלִילָה, and then dressed. As we return the Torah to the Ark we sing this beautiful prayer — עֵץ חַיִּים הִיא.

Practice reading עֵץ חַיִּים הִיא.

1   עֵץ־חַיִּים הִיא לַמַּחֲזִיקִים בָּהּ, וְתֹמְכֶיהָ מְאֻשָּׁר.

2   דְּרָכֶיהָ דַרְכֵי־נֹעַם, וְכָל־נְתִיבוֹתֶיהָ שָׁלוֹם.

It (the Torah) is a tree of life to those who uphold it and those who support it are happy. Its ways are ways of pleasantness and all its paths are peace.

Do you know the melody to עֵץ חַיִּים הִיא?

Descriptive Words

Fill in the English for these Hebrew words that describe the Torah.

חַיִּים _____

מְאֻשָּׁר _____

נֹעַם _____

שָׁלוֹם _____

עֵץ

tree

___

חַיִּים

(of) life

___

מְאֻשָּׁר

happy

___

דְּרָכֶיהָ

its ways

___

דַּרְכֵי

ways of

___

נֹעַם

pleasantness

___

שָׁלוֹם

peace

Match Game

Connect the Hebrew to its English meaning.

pleasantness	עֵץ
its ways	מְאֻשָּׁר
ways of	דְּרָכֶיהָ
happy	דַּרְכֵי
tree	נֹעַם

From the Sources

עֵץ חַיִּים הִיא is taken from the תָּנָ"ךְ (Proverbs 3). Below is the excerpt from Proverbs in which עֵץ חַיִּים הִיא is found.

Underline all the words of the עֵץ חַיִּים הִיא prayer. Then read the Biblical excerpt.

16 אֹרֶךְ יָמִים בִּימִינָהּ
בִּשְׂמֹאולָהּ עֹשֶׁר וְכָבוֹד:

17 דְּרָכֶיהָ דַרְכֵי־נֹעַם,
וְכָל־נְתִיבוֹתֶיהָ שָׁלוֹם:

18 עֵץ־חַיִּים הִיא לַמַּחֲזִיקִים בָּהּ
וְתֹמְכֶיהָ מְאֻשָּׁר:

How does the *order* of the original עֵץ חַיִּים הִיא in the תָּנָ"ךְ differ from our version in the siddur?

Prayer Building Blocks

עֵץ חַיִּים "a tree of life"

....

עֵץ   means _____

חַיִּים   means _____

Why do you think the Torah is compared to a tree?

_____

_____

Did You Know?

The two wooden rollers to which the Torah parchment is attached are also called עֲצֵי חַיִּים (the plural of עֵץ חַיִּים), trees of life.

● ● ● ● ● ● ● ● ●

עֵץ חַיִּים הִיא לַמַּחֲזִיקִים בָּה "it is a tree of life to those who uphold it"

....

Fill in the missing words in English.

The Torah is a _____ to those who uphold it.

Now fill in the missing words in Hebrew.

_____ הִיא לַמַּחֲזִיקִים בָּה.

מְאֻשָּׁר "happy"

מְאֻשָּׁר   means "happy."

אֹשֶׁר   is "happiness."

Read the following lines aloud and circle the words that have the root meaning *happy*.

How many times did you circle the word?

אַשְׁרֵי יוֹשְׁבֵי בֵיתֶךָ עוֹד יְהַלְלוּךָ סֶּלָה:

אַשְׁרֵי הָעָם שֶׁכָּכָה לּוֹ אַשְׁרֵי הָעָם שֶׁיְיָ אֱלֹהָיו:

דְּרָכֶיהָ דַרְכֵי נֹעַם "its ways are ways of pleasantness"

דְּרָכֶיהָ   means "its ways."

דַּרְכֵי   means "ways of."

Both words are variations of דֶּרֶךְ, *road* or *way*. Write the root of these words.

דְּרָכֶיהָ   דַרְכֵי

_____ _____ _____

This root means _____ or _____.

Read the two sentences below and circle the words having to do with *road* or *way*.

1   צַדִּיק יְיָ בְּכָל דְּרָכָיו, וְחָסִיד בְּכָל מַעֲשָׂיו

2   בְּשִׁבְתְּךָ בְּבֵיתֶךָ וּבְלֶכְתְּךָ בַדֶּרֶךְ וּבְשָׁכְבְּךָ וּבְקוּמֶךָ

עַל שְׁלֹשָׁה דְבָרִים

Some congregations add a special prayer before the Torah is taken out of the Ark. It comes from Pirke Avot, פִּרְקֵי אָבוֹת. It is called עַל שְׁלֹשָׁה דְבָרִים.

Practice reading the prayer below.

1 עַל־שְׁלֹשָׁה דְבָרִים הָעוֹלָם עוֹמֵד:

2 עַל הַתּוֹרָה וְעַל הָעֲבוֹדָה

3 וְעַל גְּמִילוּת חֲסָדִים.

The world stands on three things:
on Torah, worship, and acts of lovingkindness.

Fill In the Blanks

According to עַל שְׁלֹשָׁה דְבָרִים the world of Judaism stands on three pillars.

Write the English above the Hebrew below.

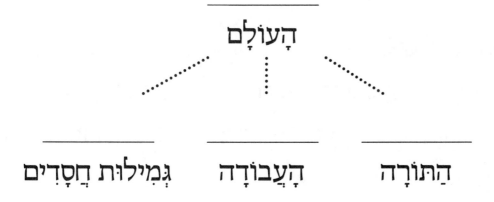

הָעוֹלָם

| גְּמִילוּת חֲסָדִים | הָעֲבוֹדָה | הַתּוֹרָה |

PRAYER DICTIONARY

עַל
on

שְׁלֹשָׁה
three

דְבָרִים
things

הָעוֹלָם
the world

עוֹמֵד
stands

הַתּוֹרָה
the Torah

הָעֲבוֹדָה
the worship

גְּמִילוּת חֲסָדִים
acts of lovingkindness

Select-A-Word

Cross out the English words that do not mean the same as the Hebrew.
Think carefully!

before	on	upon	עַל
four	one	three	שְׁלֹשָׁה
lives	nations	things	דְּבָרִים
the world	Israel	the people	הָעוֹלָם
gives	stands	makes	עוֹמֵד
the Ḥumash	the 5 Books of Moses	the Torah	הַתּוֹרָה
the worship	the praying	the Torah	הָעֲבוֹדָה
our ancestors	good deeds	acts of lovingkindness	גְּמִילוּת חֲסָדִים

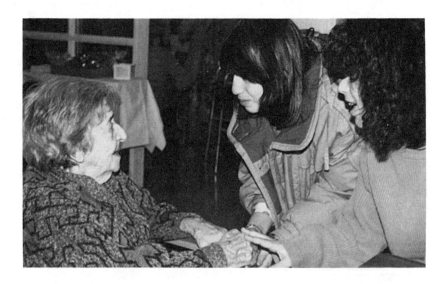

גְּמִילוּת חֲסָדִים is the performance of kind deeds. By visiting people at a home for the aged, you can help elderly people feel connected to the outside world, and you are fulfilling the mitzvah of גְּמִילוּת חֲסָדִים.

Prayer Building Blocks

עַל שְׁלֹשָׁה דְבָרִים "on three things"

. . . .

עַל   means _____.

שְׁלֹשָׁה   means _____.

Read aloud the numbers 1-10 in Hebrew, but first fill in the missing Hebrew number.

עֲשָׂרָה 10	שִׁבְעָה 7	אַרְבָּעָה 4	אֶחָד 1
	שְׁמוֹנָה 8	חֲמִשָּׁה 5	שְׁנַיִם 2
	תִּשְׁעָה 9	שִׁשָּׁה 6	_____ 3

• • • • • • • • •

דְּבָרִים   is the plural of דָּבָר.

דָּבָר   means "thing."

דְּבָרִים   means "things."

Circle the part of the word that shows it is plural.

דְּבָרִים

הָעוֹלָם עוֹמֵד "the world stands"

. . . .

הָעוֹלָם   means "the world."

הָ   means _____.

עוֹלָם   means _____.

עוֹמֵד, *stands*, has the root עמד.

The root of עֲמִידָה is _____ _____ _____.

עַל הַתּוֹרָה "on the Torah"

We know הַתּוֹרָה means "the Torah."

But הַתּוֹרָה is not just the scroll from which we read.

הַתּוֹרָה means studying the writings of the Torah and learning from it how to worship God (הָעֲבוֹדָה) and how to be a good person(גְמִילוּת חֲסָדִים).

From the Torah (הַתּוֹרָה) we learn how to act towards God (הָעֲבוֹדָה) and how to act towards other people (גְמִילוּת חֲסָדִים).

Read the בְּרָכָה that is said before studying the Torah.

בָּרוּךְ אַתָּה, יְיָ אֱלֹהֵינוּ, מֶלֶךְ הָעוֹלָם
אֲשֶׁר קִדְּשָׁנוּ בְּמִצְוֹתָיו וְצִוָּנוּ לַעֲסֹק בְּדִבְרֵי תוֹרָה.

הָעֲבוֹדָה "the worship"

הָעֲבוֹדָה	is made up of two parts.
הָ	means _____.
עֲבוֹדָה	means "worship" (or "service to God").
הָעֲבוֹדָה	means _____.

The root of עֲבוֹדָה is עבד.
The root עבד means *service* or *work*.
The service may be to God (worship) or it may be physical service (work).

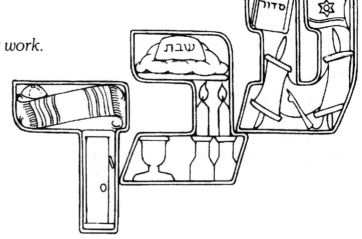

63

In each sentence below find and circle the word with the root עבד.

1. מִי שֶׁעָשָׂה נִסִּים לַאֲבוֹתֵינוּ וְגָאַל אוֹתָם מֵעַבְדוּת לְחֵרוּת.

2. הַלְלוּיָהּ; הַלְלוּ, עַבְדֵי יְיָ, הַלְלוּ אֶת שֵׁם יְיָ.

3. עַל הַתּוֹרָה, וְעַל הָעֲבוֹדָה, וְעַל הַנְּבִיאִים, וְעַל יוֹם הַשַּׁבָּת הַזֶּה.

4. וּתְהִי לְרָצוֹן תָּמִיד עֲבוֹדַת יִשְׂרָאֵל עַמֶּךָ.

5. בָּרוּךְ אַתָּה יְיָ, הַבּוֹחֵר בַּתּוֹרָה, וּבְמֹשֶׁה עַבְדּוֹ.

6. בַּעֲבוּר דָּוִד עַבְדֶּךָ, אַל תָּשֵׁב פְּנֵי מְשִׁיחֶךָ.

We worship God through prayer and by doing mitzvot.
Here are two examples of the mitzvot we do to serve God. Can you think of two more?

1. Light Shabbat candles   3. _____

2. Eat a meal in a sukkah   4. _____

גְּמִילוּת חֲסָדִים "acts of lovingkindness"

חֲסָדִים is the plural of חֶסֶד.

חֶסֶד   means a "good deed" or an "act of lovingkindness."

חֲסָדִים   means "good deeds" (plural) or "acts of lovingkindness."

Circle the part of the word that shows it is plural. חֲסָדִים

חֲסָדִים   means _____.

Here are two examples of the mitzvot we do to be good to other people.
Can you think of two more?

1. Give tzedakah   3. _____

2. Don't steal   4. _____

Fluent Reading

Each phrase contains a word you know. Practice reading the lines below.

• • • • • • • • •

1. תְּהִלַּת יְיָ יְדַבֶּר פִּי, וִיבָרֵךְ כָּל בָּשָׂר שֵׁם קָדְשׁוֹ
לְעוֹלָם וָעֶד.

2. וְדָבָר אֶחָד מִדְּבָרֶיךָ אָחוֹר לֹא יָשׁוּב רֵיקָם.

3. בֵּינִי וּבֵין בְּנֵי יִשְׂרָאֵל אוֹת הִיא לְעוֹלָם.

4. שֶׁלֹּא עָשָׂנוּ כְּגוֹיֵי הָאֲרָצוֹת וְלֹא שָׂמָנוּ
כְּמִשְׁפְּחוֹת הָאֲדָמָה.

5. שְׁלֹשָׁה מִי יוֹדֵעַ? שְׁלֹשָׁה אֲנִי יוֹדֵעַ.
שְׁלֹשָׁה אָבוֹת, שְׁנֵי לֻחוֹת הַבְּרִית,
אֶחָד אֱלֹהֵינוּ שֶׁבַּשָּׁמַיִם וּבָאָרֶץ.

6. וּלְקַיֵּם אֶת כָּל דִּבְרֵי תַלְמוּד תּוֹרָתֶךָ בְּאַהֲבָה.

7. בָּרוּךְ אַתָּה, יְיָ, גּוֹמֵל חֲסָדִים טוֹבִים לְעַמּוֹ יִשְׂרָאֵל.

65

7

עָלֵינוּ is one of the concluding prayers of every service. In this prayer we are called to praise God, and unite in harmony in our recognition of God.

• • • • • • • • •

Practice reading these lines from עָלֵינוּ.

1 עָלֵינוּ לְשַׁבֵּחַ לַאֲדוֹן הַכֹּל, לָתֵת גְּדֻלָּה לְיוֹצֵר בְּרֵאשִׁית...

2 וַאֲנַחְנוּ כּוֹרְעִים וּמִשְׁתַּחֲוִים וּמוֹדִים לִפְנֵי מֶלֶךְ
מַלְכֵי הַמְּלָכִים, הַקָּדוֹשׁ בָּרוּךְ הוּא...

3 וְנֶאֱמַר: וְהָיָה יְיָ לְמֶלֶךְ עַל־כָּל־הָאָרֶץ
בַּיּוֹם הַהוּא יִהְיֶה יְיָ אֶחָד וּשְׁמוֹ אֶחָד.

It is our duty to praise the God of all, to praise the Creator of the universe…
We bend the knee, bow, and give thanks before God,
the supreme Ruler, the Holy One, who is blessed…
And it is said: God will rule all the earth.
On that day, God will be one and God's name will be one.

Vocabulary Review

You have already learned many of the words in the עָלֵינוּ prayer.
Here is a list of familiar words in עָלֵינוּ.

11 גְּדֻלָּה	6 לְ, לַ	1 עָלֵינוּ
12 הַכֹּל (כָּל)	7 וְעַל	2 מֶלֶךְ
13 אֶחָד	8 לִפְנֵי	3 בְּרֵאשִׁית
	9 וּשְׁמוֹ (שֵׁם)	4 בָּרוּךְ
	10 הַקָּדוֹשׁ (קִדְּשָׁנוּ)	5 לָתֵת (נָתַן, וְנוֹתֵן)

In each prayer excerpt below find and underline the word(s) that appear in the list
above. Circle each word in the list as you find it in the prayer excerpt.
Now read each line.

1 בָּרוּךְ אַתָּה, יְיָ אֱלֹהֵינוּ, מֶלֶךְ הָעוֹלָם

2 הוּא יַעֲשֶׂה שָׁלוֹם עָלֵינוּ וְעַל כָּל יִשְׂרָאֵל

3 אֲשֶׁר שָׂם מֹשֶׁה לִפְנֵי בְּנֵי יִשְׂרָאֵל

4 זִכָּרוֹן לְמַעֲשֵׂה בְרֵאשִׁית

5 בָּרוּךְ אַתָּה יְיָ, נוֹתֵן הַתּוֹרָה

6 לְךָ יְיָ הַגְּדֻלָּה וְהַגְּבוּרָה

7 אֲשֶׁר קִדְּשָׁנוּ בְּמִצְוֹתָיו

8 יְיָ אֱלֹהֵינוּ, יְיָ אֶחָד

9 בָּרוּךְ שֵׁם כְּבוֹד מַלְכוּתוֹ

Word Match

Below are two lists of words:
I the list of familiar Hebrew words that appear in עָלֵינוּ
II their English equivalents

• • • • • • • • • •

Write the number of the correct Hebrew word next to its English meaning.

II		I	
_____	blessed	לְ, לַ	1
_____	greatness	לָתֵת (וְנָתַן, נוֹתֵן)	2
_____	and it is said (and say)	גְּדֻלָּה	3
_____	one	בְּרֵאשִׁית	4
_____	to	מֶלֶךְ	5
_____	Bereshit, Creation	בָּרוּךְ	6
_____	ruler	וְנֶאֱמַר (וְאָמְרוּ)	7
_____	on	עַל	8
_____	to give (gave, gives)	אֶחָד	9

Prayer Background

עָלֵינוּ is one of our most ancient prayers. We are not sure who wrote it or when, but we believe it is about 2,000 years old. In the third century C.E., עָלֵינוּ was included in the Rosh Hashanah service, and in about the 13th century it became a part of the daily prayer service. עָלֵינוּ came to be recited by Jewish men and women who, over the centuries, were put to death for refusing to convert to other religions. These Jews defiantly sang out their belief in one God and the greatness of God, and their hope for a perfect world.

Prayer Building Blocks

עָלֵינוּ לְשַׁבֵּחַ לַאֲדוֹן הַכֹּל
"It is our duty to praise the God of all"

....

עָלֵינוּ לְשַׁבֵּחַ means "it is our duty to praise."

Whom are we praising in עָלֵינוּ? _____

The word עָלֵינוּ, we have learned, means *on us* or *for us*. Do you remember this prayer?

הוּא יַעֲשֶׂה שָׁלוֹם עָלֵינוּ וְעַל כָּל יִשְׂרָאֵל

God will make peace <u>for us</u> and for all Israel.

But in the עָלֵינוּ, in order to make the sentence flow, we translate the word עָלֵינוּ as: *It is our duty (to praise).*

Dictionary words

עָלֵינוּ
it is our duty

לְשַׁבֵּחַ
to praise

לַאֲדוֹן
God

הַכֹּל
of all

וַאֲנַחְנוּ
and we

וּמוֹדִים
and thank

מֶלֶךְ מַלְכֵי הַמְּלָכִים
ruler of rulers

הָאָרֶץ
the land

בַּיוֹם הַהוּא
on that day

יִהְיֶה
will be

לַאֲדוֹן הַכֹּל "to the God of all"

....

אֲדוֹן   means "master."

הַכֹּל   means "all."

Because God is neither male nor female, we translate אֲדוֹן הַכֹּל as "God of all."

Another prayer expresses a similar idea. Do you recognize it?
Circle the word אֲדוֹן in this line.

אֲדוֹן עוֹלָם אֲשֶׁר מָלַךְ בְּטֶרֶם כָּל יְצִיר נִבְרָא.

וַאֲנַחְנוּ כּוֹרְעִים וּמִשְׁתַּחֲוִים וּמוֹדִים
"and we bend the knee and bow and thank God"

....

וַאֲנַחְנוּ   means "and we."

וַ   means _____.

אֲנַחְנוּ   means _____.

כּוֹרְעִים וּמִשְׁתַּחֲוִים means "bend the knee and bow."

וּמוֹדִים   means "and give thanks."

וּ   means _____.

מוֹדִים   means _____.

Do you know the word תּוֹדָה? Can you see the connection to the word מוֹדִים?

Find and underline the Hebrew word for *thank* in the sentences below.

1 מוֹדִים אֲנַחְנוּ לָךְ, שָׁאַתָּה הוּא יְיָ אֱלֹהֵינוּ וֵאלֹהֵי
אֲבוֹתֵינוּ לְעוֹלָם וָעֶד.

2 מוֹדֶה אֲנִי לְפָנֶיךָ, מֶלֶךְ חַי וְקַיָּם, שֶׁהֶחֱזַרְתָּ בִּי
נִשְׁמָתִי בְּחֶמְלָה, רַבָּה אֱמוּנָתֶךָ.

Circle the prefix in these words.

וּמִשְׁתַּחֲוִים   וּמוֹדִים

What does this prefix mean? _____

Bowing Skills

When reciting עָלֵינוּ, most Jews bend their knees at כּוֹרְעִים, bow slightly at
וּמִשְׁתַּחֲוִים, and stand upright at לִפְנֵי. In this way we act out the words of the
prayer.

Can you think of another prayer where we bow to God? _____

71

לִפְנֵי מֶלֶךְ מַלְכֵי הַמְּלָכִים "before the ruler of rulers"

לִפְנֵי, we have learned, means "before."
We bow down before the *ruler of rulers*.

Write the three Hebrew words that mean *ruler of rulers*.

_____ _____ _____

Each of these words has the root ____ ____ ____.

Who is מֶלֶךְ מַלְכֵי הַמְּלָכִים? _____

• • • • • • • • •

Praying Together

The suffix נוּ tells us that when we are praying we are not alone.

What does the suffix נוּ mean? _____

Below is the first part of עָלֵינוּ in its original form. Underline all the words with the suffix נוּ.

1 עָלֵינוּ לְשַׁבֵּחַ לַאֲדוֹן הַכֹּל, לָתֵת גְּדֻלָּה לְיוֹצֵר בְּרֵאשִׁית,

2 שֶׁלֹּא עָשָׂנוּ כְּגוֹיֵי הָאֲרָצוֹת וְלֹא שָׂמָנוּ כְּמִשְׁפְּחוֹת

3 הָאֲדָמָה, שֶׁלֹּא שָׂם חֶלְקֵנוּ כָּהֶם וְגֹרָלֵנוּ כְּכָל־הֲמוֹנָם.

How many words ending with נוּ did you find? _____

An Ethical Echo

In עָלֵינוּ we praise God as Creator of the universe. God's greatest creation was man and woman, whom, we are told in Genesis, were created in God's image (בְּצֶלֶם אֱלֹהִים). Since God has no physical form, "God's image" refers to the attributes or character traits we share with God.

A Point to Ponder

In your group at summer camp there is a child who is a poor athlete. When you have relay races this camper holds your team back. Since all human beings are created in God's image, how should we treat that camper?

הַקָּדוֹשׁ בָּרוּךְ הוּא "the Holy One, who is blessed"

This phrase tells us more about the *ruler of rulers*.
God is *the Holy one, who is blessed.*

Which word in the Hebrew phrase means *holy*? _____

Write the root of this word. _____ _____ _____

Which word means *blessed*? _____

Write the root of this word. _____ _____ _____

וְנֶאֱמַר: וְהָיָה יְיָ לְמֶלֶךְ עַל כָּל הָאָרֶץ
"and it is said: God will rule all the earth"

This line tells us יְיָ will be מֶלֶךְ עַל כָּל הָאָרֶץ.

מֶלֶךְ   means _____.

עַל   means _____.

כָּל   means _____.

הָאָרֶץ   means "the land."

הָ   means _____.

אָרֶץ   means _____.

Complete the phrase in Hebrew

וְנֶאֱמַר: וְהָיָה יְיָ _____ עַל כָּל _____

73

בַּיּוֹם הַהוּא יִהְיֶה יְיָ אֶחָד וּשְׁמוֹ אֶחָד
"on that day, God will be one and God's name will be one"

....

בַּיּוֹם הַהוּא   means "on that day."

יוֹם   means "day."

Read the names of the days of the week in Hebrew.
Fill in the missing English word.

יוֹם חֲמִישִׁי	יוֹם רְבִיעִי	יוֹם שְׁלִישִׁי	יוֹם שֵׁנִי	יוֹם רִאשׁוֹן
Thursday	Wednesday	Tuesday	Monday	Sunday

יוֹם שִׁשִּׁי	יוֹם שַׁבָּת
_____	Friday

One of the ways we show that we were created in God's image is by performing God's mitzvot. By recycling paper, these children are helping to preserve the environment and fulfill the mitzvah of בַּל תַּשְׁחִית ("do not destroy").

Fluent Reading

Each phrase contains a word you know. Practice reading the lines below.

• • • • • • • • •

1. אֵל חַי וְקַיָּם תָּמִיד יִמְלֹךְ עָלֵינוּ לְעוֹלָם וָעֶד.

2. רֹאשׁ חֹדֶשׁ... יִהְיֶה בְּיוֹם... הַבָּא עָלֵינוּ וְעַל כָּל יִשְׂרָאֵל לְטוֹבָה.

3. יְחַדְּשֵׁהוּ הַקָּדוֹשׁ בָּרוּךְ הוּא עָלֵינוּ.

4. אֵל אָדוֹן עַל כָּל הַמַּעֲשִׂים.

5. וַאֲנִי אֶשְׁתַּחֲוֶה וְאֶכְרָעָה, אֲבָרְכָה לִפְנֵי יְיָ עֹשִׂי.

6. מוֹדִים אֲנַחְנוּ לָךְ עַל חַיֵּינוּ הַמְּסוּרִים בְּיָדֶךָ.

7. שָׁלוֹם עֲלֵיכֶם, מַלְאֲכֵי הַשָּׁרֵת, מַלְאֲכֵי עֶלְיוֹן מִמֶּלֶךְ מַלְכֵי הַמְּלָכִים, הַקָּדוֹשׁ בָּרוּךְ הוּא.

8. בָּרוּךְ אַתָּה יְיָ עַל הָאָרֶץ וְעַל הַמָּזוֹן.

9. הָאֵל הַמֶּלֶךְ הַגָּדוֹל וְהַקָּדוֹשׁ בַּשָּׁמַיִם וּבָאָרֶץ.

10. וְהוּא הָיָה וְהוּא הֹוֶה וְהוּא יִהְיֶה בְּתִפְאָרָה.

75

8

The קַדִּישׁ prayer appears in every prayer service. There are five versions of the קַדִּישׁ. The קַדִּישׁ we will study in this lesson comes near the end of the service. It is called the Mourner's Kaddish.

* * * * * * * * *

Practice reading the Mourner's Kaddish.

1 יִתְגַּדַּל וְיִתְקַדַּשׁ שְׁמֵהּ רַבָּא

2 בְּעָלְמָא דִּי בְרָא כִרְעוּתֵהּ, וְיַמְלִיךְ מַלְכוּתֵהּ

3 בְּחַיֵּיכוֹן וּבְיוֹמֵיכוֹן וּבְחַיֵּי דְכָל־בֵּית יִשְׂרָאֵל,

4 בַּעֲגָלָא וּבִזְמַן קָרִיב, וְאִמְרוּ אָמֵן.

5 יְהֵא שְׁמֵהּ רַבָּא מְבָרַךְ לְעָלַם וּלְעָלְמֵי עָלְמַיָּא.

6 יִתְבָּרַךְ וְיִשְׁתַּבַּח וְיִתְפָּאַר וְיִתְרוֹמַם וְיִתְנַשֵּׂא

7 וְיִתְהַדָּר וְיִתְעַלֶּה וְיִתְהַלָּל שְׁמֵהּ דְּקֻדְשָׁא, בְּרִיךְ הוּא.

8 לְעֵלָּא מִן כָּל־בִּרְכָתָא וְשִׁירָתָא,

9 תֻּשְׁבְּחָתָא וְנֶחֱמָתָא דַּאֲמִירָן בְּעָלְמָא, וְאִמְרוּ אָמֵן.

10 יְהֵא שְׁלָמָא רַבָּא מִן שְׁמַיָּא

11 וְחַיִּים עָלֵינוּ וְעַל־כָּל־יִשְׂרָאֵל, וְאִמְרוּ אָמֵן.

12 עֹשֶׂה שָׁלוֹם בִּמְרוֹמָיו הוּא יַעֲשֶׂה שָׁלוֹם

13 עָלֵינוּ וְעַל־כָּל־יִשְׂרָאֵל, וְאִמְרוּ אָמֵן.

May God's name be great and may it be made holy
in the world created according to God's will. May God rule
in our own lives and our own days, and in the life of all the house of Israel,
swiftly and soon and say, Amen.
May God's great name be blessed forever and ever.
Blessed, praised, glorified, exalted, extolled,
honored, magnified, and adored be the name of the Holy One blessed is God,
though God is beyond all the blessings, songs,
adorations and consolations that are spoken in the world, and say, Amen.
May there be great peace from heaven
and life for us and for all Israel, and say, Amen.
God who makes peace in the heavens will make peace
for us and for all Israel. And say, Amen.

Did You Know?

Did you notice something different about the language of the קַדִּישׁ?

Most of the words are Aramaic. Aramaic was the language spoken by the Jews at the time of Ezra in the fifth century B.C.E. and for hundreds of years thereafter. The last two lines of the קַדִּישׁ are written in Hebrew. Do you recognize them?

True or False

Put a ✔ in the box if the statement is true; leave it blank if the statement is false.

☐ **1.** The קַדִּישׁ called the Mourner's Kaddish comes near the end of every service.

☐ **2.** There are two versions of the קַדִּישׁ.

☐ **3.** Most of the קַדִּישׁ is written in Aramaic.

☐ **4.** Our ancestors spoke Aramaic instead of Hebrew for many centuries.

☐ **5.** The last lines of the קַדִּישׁ speak about *peace*.

קַדִּישׁ
holy

יִתְגַּדֵּל
will be great

וְיִתְקַדֵּשׁ
and will be holy

שְׁמֵהּ
(God's) name

בְּעָלְמָא
in the world

וְיַמְלִיךְ
and will rule

מַלְכוּתֵהּ
kingdom

The Hebrew-Aramaic Connection

In the right hand column are Hebrew prayer words you have learned.

Write the number of the Hebrew word next to the related Aramaic word from the קַדִּישׁ. (Hint: Look for related roots.)

ARAMAIC		HEBREW	
בְּרִיךְ	____	גְּדָלָה	1
בְּעָלְמָא	____	קִדְּשָׁנוּ	2
וּבְחַיֵּי	____	הָעוֹלָם	3
יִתְגַּדַּל	____	מֶלֶךְ	4
קַדִּישׁ, וְיִתְקַדַּשׁ	____	חַיִּים	5
וְיַמְלִיךְ	____	בָּרוּךְ	6
שְׁלָמָא	____	שָׁלוֹם	7

Prayer Dictionary sidebar:

וּבְחַיֵּי
and in the life of

לְעָלַם
forever

וְיִשְׁתַּבַּח
and will be praised

בְּרִיךְ
blessed

בִּרְכָתָא
blessings

שְׁלָמָא
peace

Although these words may look difficult, in fact, you know them all!

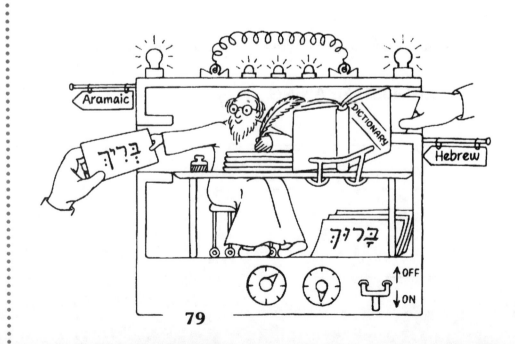

79

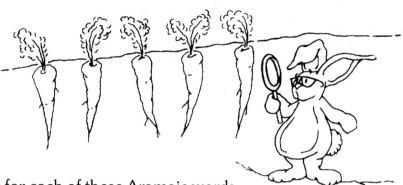

Root Search

Write the שֹׁרֶשׁ (root) for each of these Aramaic words.

ROOT	ARAMAIC WORD
—— —— ——	בְּרִיךְ
—— —— ——	מַלְכוּתֵהּ
—— —— ——	יִתְגַּדַּל
—— —— ——	בִּרְכָתָא
—— —— ——	וְיַמְלִיךְ
—— —— ——	קַדִּישׁ, (וְיִתְקַדַּשׁ)
—— —— ——	שְׁלָמָא

Choose any four roots and write the English meaning.

ENGLISH MEANING	ROOT
_____	—— —— ——
_____	—— —— ——
_____	—— —— ——
_____	—— —— ——

Word Match

Draw a line from the Aramaic word to its English meaning.

forever   קַדִּישׁ

kingdom   בְּרִיךְ

holy   לְעָלַם

blessed   מַלְכוּתֵהּ

---

name   שְׁלָמָא

and will be praised   שְׁמֵהּ

will be great   וְיִשְׁתַּבַּח

peace   יִתְגַּדַּל

---

and will be holy   בִּרְכָתָא

and will rule   וּבְחַיֵּי

blessings   וְיַמְלִיךְ

and in the life of   וְיִתְקַדַּשׁ

Kaddish Search

Read the קַדִּיש and find the solutions to the questions on the opposite page.

1   יִתְגַּדַּל וְיִתְקַדַּשׁ שְׁמֵהּ רַבָּא

2   בְּעָלְמָא דִּי בְרָא כִרְעוּתֵהּ, וְיַמְלִיךְ מַלְכוּתֵהּ

3   בְּחַיֵּיכוֹן וּבְיוֹמֵיכוֹן וּבְחַיֵּי דְכָל־בֵּית יִשְׂרָאֵל,

4   בַּעֲגָלָא וּבִזְמַן קָרִיב, וְאִמְרוּ אָמֵן.

5   יְהֵא שְׁמֵהּ רַבָּא מְבָרַךְ לְעָלַם וּלְעָלְמֵי עָלְמַיָּא.

6   יִתְבָּרַךְ וְיִשְׁתַּבַּח וְיִתְפָּאַר וְיִתְרוֹמַם וְיִתְנַשֵּׂא

7   וְיִתְהַדָּר וְיִתְעַלֶּה וְיִתְהַלָּל שְׁמֵהּ דְּקֻדְשָׁא, בְּרִיךְ הוּא.

8   לְעֵלָּא מִן כָּל־בִּרְכָתָא וְשִׁירָתָא,

9   תֻּשְׁבְּחָתָא וְנֶחֱמָתָא דַּאֲמִירָן בְּעָלְמָא, וְאִמְרוּ אָמֵן.

10   יְהֵא שְׁלָמָא רַבָּא מִן שְׁמַיָּא

11   וְחַיִּים עָלֵינוּ וְעַל־כָּל־יִשְׂרָאֵל, וְאִמְרוּ אָמֵן.

12   עֹשֶׂה שָׁלוֹם בִּמְרוֹמָיו הוּא יַעֲשֶׂה שָׁלוֹם

13   עָלֵינוּ וְעַל־כָּל־יִשְׂרָאֵל, וְאִמְרוּ אָמֵן.

1. (Circle) all the words in the קַדִּישׁ that have the root קדשׁ.

    How many words did you circle?_____

    What does the root קדשׁ mean?_____

2. Put a ✡ above all the words with the root ברכ.

    How many words did you star?_____

    What does the root ברכ mean?_____

3. Three words in the קַדִּישׁ mean *life*. Write them here.

    _____ _____ _____

4. *Peace* is an important concept in the קַדִּישׁ. Write the Hebrew word for

    *peace.*_____

    This word — or a variation — appears 3 times near the end of the קַדִּישׁ.

    Put a |square| around each one.

5. We know that כָּל means _____.

    Now <u>underline</u> כָּל or כָּל whenever it appears.

    How many underlined words do you have?_____

6. עוֹלָם means *forever* or *world*. This word appears 5 times, in a variety of
    forms, in the קַדִּישׁ.

    Write the 5 words here.

    _____ _____ _____ _____ _____

About the Kaddish

There are different versions of the קַדִּישׁ in the סִדּוּר. The קַדִּישׁ divides up the service. Think of it as a file divider that separates the subjects in your school binder. The קַדִּישׁ indicates the end of one section of the service and the beginning of the next.

We are not sure who wrote the קַדִּישׁ or when. It probably developed over hundreds of years. We do know that almost 800 years ago the קַדִּישׁ became the prayer said by mourners.

The Mourner's Kaddish is said in memory of someone who has died. In some congregations only the mourners stand as they recite the קַדִּישׁ; in other congregations everyone stands to say קַדִּישׁ.

As the mourners rhythmically chant its words, they feel a sense of comfort and reassurance. Although the Mourner's Kaddish is recited in memory of the dead, its words give strength to the living.

• • • • • • • • •

Phrase Match

Write the number of the siddur phrase next to the English phrase that has the same meaning.

____ will be blessed and will be praised	יִתְגַּדַּל וְיִתְקַדַּשׁ שְׁמֵהּ רַבָּא	1
____ and in the life of all the House of Israel	וְיַמְלִיךְ מַלְכוּתֵהּ	2
____ God will make peace	וּבְחַיֵּי דְכָל־בֵּית יִשְׂרָאֵל	3
____ may God's name be great and holy	לְעָלַם וּלְעָלְמֵי עָלְמַיָּא	4
____ and rule God's kingdom	יִתְבָּרַךְ וְיִשְׁתַּבַּח	5
____ forever and ever	הוּא יַעֲשֶׂה שָׁלוֹם	6

84

The Theme of the Prayer

We have learned that the Mourner's Kaddish is said in memory of someone who has died. But did you know that the קַדִּישׁ contains no mention of death?

● ● ● ● ● ● ● ● ●

Reread the English translation of the קַדִּישׁ at the beginning of this lesson. Pay attention to the tone and mood of the prayer. Then answer the following questions.

1. Fill in the blank by choosing the correct word.

The קַדִּישׁ is a prayer of _____ to God. (thanks/praise/request)

2. Choose 4 words from the English translation of the prayer that illustrate your answer to Question 1.

_____ _____ _____ _____

3. The קַדִּישׁ ends on a hopeful, optimistic note.

It ends with a wish for _____.

4. Why do you think the קַדִּישׁ is recited by mourners even though it does not mention death?

_____

_____

_____

Below are the last two lines of the קַדִּישׁ.

עֹשֶׂה שָׁלוֹם בִּמְרוֹמָיו הוּא יַעֲשֶׂה שָׁלוֹם

עָלֵינוּ וְעַל־כָּל־יִשְׂרָאֵל, וְאִמְרוּ אָמֵן.

Do you recall another place in the סִדּוּר where these lines appear?

Read these two words and write the שֹׁרֶשׁ.

עֹשֶׂה   יַעֲשֶׂה

_____ _____ _____

What does this root mean? _____

Answer the questions *in Hebrew*:

1. In עֲשֵׂה שָׁלוֹם what do we ask God for?

_____

2. For whom do we want peace?

_____

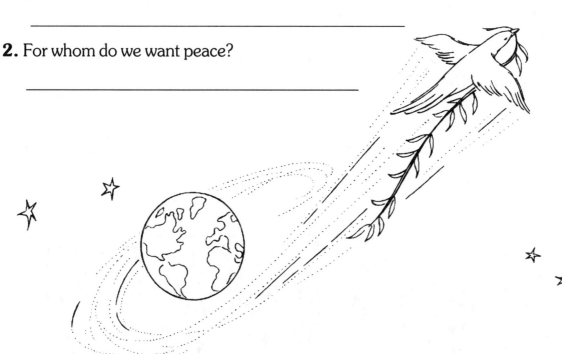

Fluent Reading

Each phrase contains a word you know. Practice reading the lines below.

• • • • • • • • •

1. תִּתְגַּדֵּל וְתִתְקַדֵּשׁ בְּתוֹךְ יְרוּשָׁלַיִם עִירְךָ.

2. לְדוֹר וָדוֹר נַגִּיד גָּדְלֶךָ, וּלְנֵצַח נְצָחִים קְדֻשָּׁתְךָ נַקְדִּישׁ.

3. גָּדוֹל יְיָ וּמְהֻלָּל מְאֹד וְלִגְדֻלָּתוֹ אֵין חֵקֶר.

4. וְשִׁבְחֲךָ אֱלֹהֵינוּ מִפִּינוּ לֹא יָמוּשׁ לְעוֹלָם וָעֶד.

5. עָלֵינוּ לְשַׁבֵּחַ לַאֲדוֹן הַכֹּל לָתֵת גְּדֻלָּה לְיוֹצֵר בְּרֵאשִׁית.

6. יִגְדַּל אֱלֹהִים חַי וְיִשְׁתַּבַּח.

7. מַלְכוּתְךָ מַלְכוּת כָּל עֹלָמִים, וּמֶמְשַׁלְתְּךָ בְּכָל דּוֹר וָדֹר.

8. הַבָּא עָלֵינוּ וְעַל כָּל יִשְׂרָאֵל לְטוֹבָה.

9. עֹשֶׂה שָׁלוֹם בִּמְרוֹמָיו הוּא יַעֲשֶׂה שָׁלוֹם עָלֵינוּ
   וְעַל־כָּל־יִשְׂרָאֵל.

10. כִּי הַמַּלְכוּת שֶׁלְּךָ הִיא וּלְעוֹלְמֵי עַד תִּמְלֹךְ בְּכָבוֹד.

11. בָּרְכוּנִי לְשָׁלוֹם מַלְאֲכֵי הַשָּׁלוֹם מַלְאֲכֵי עֶלְיוֹן.

At the end of Shabbat and holiday services, we sing a song that is familiar to Jews throughout the world; a song with simple words and an easy tune; a song that makes an important statement about our belief in God: אֵין כֵּאלֹהֵינוּ — There is None Like Our God!

Practice reading אֵין כֵּאלֹהֵינוּ.

אֵין כֵּאלֹהֵינוּ,	אֵין כַּאדוֹנֵינוּ,	1
אֵין כְּמַלְכֵּנוּ,	אֵין כְּמוֹשִׁיעֵנוּ.	2
מִי כֵאלֹהֵינוּ	מִי כַאדוֹנֵינוּ,	3
מִי כְמַלְכֵּנוּ,	מִי כְמוֹשִׁיעֵנוּ.	4
נוֹדֶה לֵאלֹהֵינוּ,	נוֹדֶה לַאדוֹנֵינוּ	5
נוֹדֶה לְמַלְכֵּנוּ,	נוֹדֶה לְמוֹשִׁיעֵנוּ.	6
בָּרוּךְ אֱלֹהֵינוּ,	בָּרוּךְ אֲדוֹנֵינוּ,	7
בָּרוּךְ מַלְכֵּנוּ,	בָּרוּךְ מוֹשִׁיעֵנוּ.	8
אַתָּה הוּא אֱלֹהֵינוּ,	אַתָּה הוּא אֲדוֹנֵינוּ,	9
אַתָּה הוּא מַלְכֵּנוּ,	אַתָּה הוּא מוֹשִׁיעֵנוּ.	10

There is none like our God,
There is none like our Ruler,
Who is like our God?
Who is like our Ruler?
We will give thanks to our God.
We will give thanks to our Ruler.
Blessed is our God.
Blessed is our Ruler.
You are our God.
You are our Ruler.

There is none like our Sovereign
There is none like our Savior.
Who is like our Sovereign?
Who is like our Savior?
We will give thanks to our Sovereign.
We will give thanks to our Savior.
Blessed is our Sovereign.
Blessed is our Savior.
You are our Sovereign.
You are our Savior.

Search and Circle

Circle the Hebrew word that means the same as the English.

English			
our Savior	אָבִינוּ	אֱלֹהֵינוּ	מוֹשִׁיעֵנוּ
There is none like	בָּרוּךְ שֶׁ	אֵין כּ	אַתָּה הוּא
our Sovereign	אֲדוֹנֵינוּ	אֱלֹהֵינוּ	אֲבוֹתֵינוּ
our Ruler	מַלְכֵּנוּ	קִדְּשָׁנוּ	אֱלֹהֵינוּ
we will give thanks to	בָּרְכוּ אֶת	נוֹדֶה ל	לְעַמּוֹ
you are	יְיָ אֶחָד	אַתָּה הוּא	עָלֵינוּ
our God	מַלְכוּתוֹ	וְצִוָּנוּ	אֱלֹהֵינוּ
who is like?	כִּי בָנוּ	לְעוֹלָם וָעֶד	מִי כּ

אֵין כּ
there is none like

מִי כּ
who is like

נוֹדֶה ל
we will give thanks to

אַתָּה הוּא
you are

אֱלֹהֵינוּ
our God

אֲדוֹנֵינוּ
our Sovereign

מַלְכֵּנוּ
our Ruler

מוֹשִׁיעֵנוּ
our Savior

Architecture of the Prayer

See how carefully structured אֵין כֵּאלֹהֵינוּ is.

• • • • • • • • •

Read the prayer across (◀) line by line, then complete the activities below.

1	אֵין כֵּאלֹהֵינוּ, אֵין כַּאדוֹנֵינוּ,
2	אֵין כְּמַלְכֵּנוּ, אֵין כְּמוֹשִׁיעֵנוּ.
3	מִי כֵאלֹהֵינוּ, מִי כַאדוֹנֵינוּ,
4	מִי כְמַלְכֵּנוּ, מִי כְמוֹשִׁיעֵנוּ.
5	נוֹדֶה לֵאלֹהֵינוּ, נוֹדֶה לַאדוֹנֵינוּ,
6	נוֹדֶה לְמַלְכֵּנוּ, נוֹדֶה לְמוֹשִׁיעֵנוּ.
7	בָּרוּךְ אֱלֹהֵינוּ, בָּרוּךְ אֲדוֹנֵינוּ,
8	בָּרוּךְ מַלְכֵּנוּ, בָּרוּךְ מוֹשִׁיעֵנוּ.
9	אַתָּה הוּא אֱלֹהֵינוּ, אַתָּה הוּא אֲדוֹנֵינוּ,
10	אַתָּה הוּא מַלְכֵּנוּ, אַתָּה הוּא מוֹשִׁיעֵנוּ.

1. Circle אֵין each time it appears.

2. Underline מִי each time it appears.

3. Put a box around נוֹדֶה each time it appears.

The Secret Word

אֵין כֵּאלֹהֵינוּ is an acrostic. In an acrostic the initial letters of certain words spell out a new "secret" word.

Circle the first letter of the Hebrew words below from אֵין כֵּאלֹהֵינוּ.

אֵין מִי נוֹדֶה

Write the 3 letters in the spaces below.
(Remember "נ" at the end of a word is written "ן".)

_____ _____ _____

Did you figure out the secret word?
When do we say this word?

Prayer Building Blocks

The Suffix נוּ

....

אֱלֹהֵינוּ   means "our God."

מַלְכֵּנוּ   means "our Ruler."

מוֹשִׁיעֵנוּ   means "our Savior."

All of these words describing God end with the suffix _____.

Underline the suffix in each of the above words.

What does this suffix mean? _____

אֵין כְ "there is none like"

אֵין   means "there is none."

כְ   is a prefix that means "like."

אֵין כְ   means _____.

Circle the Hebrew word and prefix meaning "there is none like" in the lines below.

אֵין כֵּאלֹהֵינוּ   אֵין כַּאדוֹנֵינוּ

אֵין כְּמַלְכֵּנוּ   אֵין כְּמוֹשִׁיעֵנוּ

מִי כְ "who is like?"

מִי   means "who is?"

כְ   means "like"

Circle the word and prefix meaning "who is like?" in each of the lines below.

מִי כֵאלֹהֵינוּ   מִי כַאדוֹנֵינוּ

מִי כְמַלְכֵּנוּ   מִי כְמוֹשִׁיעֵנוּ

נוֹדֶה לְ "we will give thanks to"

נוֹדֶה   means "we will give thanks."

לְ   is a prefix that means _____.

Circle the Hebrew word and prefix meaning "we will give thanks to" in the lines below.

נוֹדֶה לֵאלֹהֵינוּ   נוֹדֶה לַאדוֹנֵינוּ

נוֹדֶה לְמַלְכֵּנוּ   נוֹדֶה לְמוֹשִׁיעֵנוּ

Prefix Review

In אֵין כֵּאלֹהֵינוּ two prefixes are repeated. They are כְּ and לְ. Circle the prefix in each of these words.

כֵּאלֹהֵינוּ   לַאדוֹנֵינוּ   לְמַלְכֵּנוּ   כְּמוֹשִׁיעֵנוּ

Write the meaning of each prefix.

כְּ _____

לְ _____

אַתָּה הוּא "You are"

Circle the Hebrew words that mean "You are" in the lines below.

אַתָּה הוּא אֱלֹהֵינוּ   אַתָּה הוּא אֲדוֹנֵינוּ

אַתָּה הוּא מַלְכֵּנוּ   אַתָּה הוּא מוֹשִׁיעֵנוּ

• • • • • • • • •

Prayer Concept

אֵין כֵּאלֹהֵינוּ was written some time before the 9th century. It is over 1,000 years old! אֵין כֵּאלֹהֵינוּ is an important statement of our belief in God.

Reread the English translation of אֵין כֵּאלֹהֵינוּ at the beginning of the chapter. In your own words, describe the Jewish attitude towards God that is expressed in אֵין כֵּאלֹהֵינוּ.

Putting It Together

You know the beginning (prefix) and the ending (suffix) of each word below.

◯   ◯   ◯   ◯

כְּמוֹשִׁיעֵנוּ   לְמַלְכֵּנוּ   לַאדוֹנֵינוּ   כֵּאלהֵינוּ

Write the number of the correct English meaning above each Hebrew word.

     1. to our Ruler
     2. to our Sovereign
     3. like our Savior
     4. like our God

Now circle the "main part" (not prefix or suffix) of each Hebrew word above. The first one is done for you.

• • • • • • • • •

Each of these "main parts" is an important word. When a word has a prefix or suffix added, it may change its vowels or lose a final letter.

Connect the "real word" in column 1 with the changed "main part" in column 2.

2	1	
אֱלֹהֵי	מֶלֶךְ	_____
מַלְכֵּ	אָדוֹן	_____
אֲדוֹנִי	מוֹשִׁיעַ	_____
מוֹשִׁיעַ	אֱלֹהִים	_____

Now fill in the English meaning for the words in column 1 in the blank spaces above.

94

Fluent Reading

Each phrase contains a word you know. Practice reading the lines below.

● ● ● ● ● ● ● ● ●

1 מִי כַּיְיָ אֱלֹהֵינוּ, הַמַּגְבִּיהִי לָשָׁבֶת.

2 אָבִינוּ מַלְכֵּנוּ, שְׁמַע קוֹלֵנוּ.

3 אֵין גְּדוֹלָה כַּתּוֹרָה וְאֵין דוֹרְשֶׁיהָ כְּיִשְׂרָאֵל.

4 הוּא מַלְכֵּנוּ. הוּא מוֹשִׁיעֵנוּ.

5 בָּרְכֵנוּ אָבִינוּ כֻּלָּנוּ כְּאֶחָד בְּאוֹר פָּנֶיךָ.

6 אֵין אַדִּיר כַּיְיָ, וְאֵין בָּרוּךְ כְּבֶן עַמְרָם.

7 אֶחָד הוּא אֱלֹהֵינוּ. הוּא אָבִינוּ.

8 בָּרוּךְ אַתָּה, יְיָ אֱלֹהֵינוּ, מֶלֶךְ הָעוֹלָם,
   הָאֵל, אָבִינוּ, מַלְכֵּנוּ.

9 אָבִינוּ מַלְכֵּנוּ, חַדֵּשׁ עָלֵינוּ שָׁנָה טוֹבָה.

Conclusion

"Hebrew is the link that unites us with millions of worshippers."

You are one of the millions of worshippers referred to in the words above. Now that you are familiar with the most important prayers in the Shabbat Morning Service and the Friday Evening Service, you are united in a new way with the Jewish people. Not only are you able to pray with Jews in your own congregation, but with Jews throughout America, and the entire world. Jews who speak a different language than you—French, Spanish, German—pray in the same language as you—Hebrew. The *Shema* you recite on Friday is being recited by Jews in Mexico, Brazil, Australia, England, and of course, Israel.

Most importantly, you are now ready to be an active participant in your own synagogue. You can read the prayers, you have studied the key prayer vocabulary, and you have discussed the ethical values associated with each one. Go and make your congregation, and the Jewish community, a stronger one.

May you go from strength to strength.

חֲזַק חֲזַק וְנִתְחַזֵּק